FLICKA'S FRIEND

FLICKA'S FRIEND

The Autobiography of
Mary O'Hara

G. P. Putnam's Sons
New York

Copyright © 1982 by Markane Company, Inc.
All rights reserved. This book, or parts thereof, may not be
reproduced in any form without permission. Published
in Canada by General Publishing Co. Limited, Toronto

All photographs in this book are from Mary O'Hara's personal
collection except for the following: Mary at Remount (sitting at her
typewriter), courtesy of the American Heritage Center, University of
Wyoming; Mary in library, courtesy of Marian Stephenson.

Library of Congress Cataloging in Publication Data

O'Hara, Mary.
    Flicka's friend.

    1. O'Hara, Mary—Biography. 2. Authors, American—
20th century—Biography. I. Title.
PS3529.H34Z465 1982   813'.52[B]   81-22665
ISBN 0-399-12727-5   921   AACR2

PRINTED IN THE UNITED STATES OF AMERICA

Contents

PART TWO

PART THREE

CONTENTS

PART FOUR

next morning

After breakfast ^Rob went down to the nursery to see Flicka.
Nell left her dishes and went too, with Pauly on her shoulder.
Howard and Ken were already there.

Flicka had eaten her breakfast oats and licked the box clean.
She lifted her head with ease, she whinnied now and then, but
she would not get up.

Rob, whose eyes made observations with the speed and precision,
of ~~a machine~~, said, " Stand back, all of you-- I'm going to
roll her over ~~on~~ *to* the other side. "

Flicka was lying on her left side. He went behind her, leaned
over, got hold of ~~both of~~ her left legs, one in his left hand,
one in his right, then, backing off, he gently hauled her over
until she was lying on her right side.

Flicka immediately made a scramble, using her two fore~~feet~~ *legs*
and the left hind leg to push with, and got up. Everyone ~~began~~
~~to~~ laugh *ed*. Flicka stood calmly in the centre of the group, and
when Ken went to her head and put his hands on either side of
her face, she remained quiet.

"Nothing wrong with her back," said McLaughlin. " It's her
leg. That right hind leg. She couldn't use it to push with,
and, lying on the left side, she couldn't get up without it. "

"But she's been using it, Dad," said Ken anxiously. *now*

"Yes. It was healed ~~up some time ago.~~ But look at it, It's
swollen. That means infection, and it hurts her ~~now~~ worse than
~~when~~ *did at* it ~~was~~ first, ~~out.~~ Look, she's not bearing her weight
on it. "

Ken's face looked distraught when he noticed the swelling
above the joint. Everyone knew that the worst danger of wire
cuts was the infection that so often followed. " What do you

Prologue

Iam beginning this autobiography on my ninetieth birthday.

I was destined to be a writer. I might almost say predestined, for I wrote my first short story when I was seven. The title was "Lonely Laurie." As soon as it was finished I wrote another, and since then have never stopped writing.

When I was fifty-six I wrote a story that became famous, "My Friend Flicka," and ever since, people have been asking questions about the author. How did I do it? Where did I get my ideas? So I am undertaking this autobiography—to answer all the questions.

It will be hard for me. Heretofore, I have let my imagination have full play, as every writer of fiction does and must do. Now this is forbidden, and I must depend on facts. Fortunately I have a good memory. It is as if every deed, word, expression and gesture is recorded somewhere within me and can be recalled if I sink deep enough, concentrate, wait for it.

As a child I was noted for always having (and demanding from others) the "very words."

However, to relate the happenings of a life which has already lasted more than ninety years is impossible. I must make a selection. I will tell of my romances and marriages. I will tell of my background, my parents and siblings, my home and travels, my teachers. In my stories about horses I never shirked the scenes of the little foals coming to birth so I will not exclude the birth scenes of my own little foals.

I will tell of my work and work methods. One often hears of outstanding success being achieved by complete dedication to that single ambition and a dogged perseverance in pursuing it. I had no such grandiose hope. My wishes were much more humble. I wanted to be pretty and lovable and attractive so that, when I was of marriageable age, some man would propose to me and I could get married and have children and then, like all the heroines in the storybooks, live happily ever after.

PART ONE

PART ONE

1

Beginnings

I was born on July 10, 1885, the third of four children, to an Episcopalian clergyman, the Reverend Dr. Reese F. Alsop, and Mary Lee (née Spring) Alsop. Elma, my sister, was the oldest child, followed by Reese, myself, and my younger sister Bess.

I was named after my maternal grandmother, Mary O'Hara Spring, née Denny, and her family, the Dennys, had practically the same history as the city of Pittsburgh.

Back in the days when land was a few dollars an acre the Dennys and O'Haras had bought hundreds of acres at the junction of three great rivers, the Ohio, the Allegheny and the Monongahela. The city of Pittsburgh slowly rose upon those acres. Anyone owning them had only to hold on to become very rich indeed.

The Dennys held on.

The Denny Estate was as well known in Pittsburgh as the Astor Estate was in New York. We knew, as most children do, just what worldly goods would come to us by inheritance when we grew up. And even though the legacy would be divided at first in two parts between grandmother's two daughters, and then one of them subdivided into four parts for the four of us, it would be lots of money and we would be rich.

My grandmother's home was a thousand-acre tract fifty miles from Pittsburgh. A little spur of the railroad ran out to a specially built "Denny Station" for her convenience. The Denny Station was close to the great muddy flood of the Allegheny River. A mile inland was the stately white-pillared mansion surrounded by original Denny woodland turned park and farm.

This was Deercreek, where we children spent our summers and collected memories that are probably the happiest of our lives. For there were saddle horses and a pony to ride, farm horses to straddle when they were driven for loads of gravel or loam, an outdoor playground with swimming pool and a tennis court, a herd of Jersey cows for milk and cream, and miles of woodland for us to wander in.

And there were always a gang of cousins from town visiting us. And it was all our very own because we were Dennys.

My grandmother was one of those rare beings about whom it can be said all who knew her loved her. I adored her. Wherever she went, she was the outstanding personage, like a sovereign. She liked traveling, and when the winter snows descended on New England, would go abroad, moving from one fashionable watering place to the other.

That she was suspected of being "consumptive," of having weak lungs, was not apparent except as an air of extreme delicacy or fragility. Grandma May was seldom sick in bed but nearly always under the watchful eye of a good doctor.

On trips she liked to have Elma and Bess and me accompany her. Sometimes our father would let us leave our schools in Brooklyn and go with her. Travel abroad was considered an important part of the education of young ladies.

We stayed at the grand hotels. At teatime at one hotel a band played in the bandstand. Small tables and chairs were conveniently set along the edge of the colonnade which separated the hotel from the gardens. Here, hotel guests would gather to sip tea or aperitifs, chatter, watch and comment.

When my grandmother appeared to make her way down the long walk, people would turn or move up to watch her, and whisper, "Who is she? Who is she?" Slender and of medium height, always dressed in black, she never lost her erect posture or the regal carriage of her beautiful head. Her white hair was covered with white lace. Her clear blue eyes looked steadily forward, kindly, but reserved and apart.

At her right, with a hand supporting her elbow, was Signorina de Thierry from Switzerland. At her left, Fraulein von Raabe from Poland. Close behind her, her three granddaughters.

We resembled each other, all being about the same height, all with dark brown hair cut in bangs to our eyebrows in front and swinging in thick curls to our waists in back. The curls were glossy ringlets insisted on by Grandma May, the result of much labor night and morning by our maid.

In character, we were quite different. Elma was a clown, determined to be funny in everything she said and did and make everyone laugh. I was shy, reserved and silent. But I could be drawn out and had plenty of words if there was good conversation, witty words with a bite to them. Bess had no words at all but knew she did not need them. She was simply stunning.

As we walked down the colonnade side by side behind our grandmother, our governess, walking stiffly beside us, kept her eyes ahead as if to direct us to do the same; but we were aware of the commotion that our procession made, and that not all the admiring glances were for our grandmother.

A good many came our way, as well as some frank smiles.
"Oue occhi!"

A talent for music almost amounting to genius ran in
our family, cropping out somewhere in every generation. A
baby would stop crying, turn its head, listen with a
changed expression when music began. By the time it was
four years old it would be recognized as "the musical one."

I had hardly passed my first birthday when my mother
was announcing that I was going to be one of the musical
Dennys, insisting that she could tell it by my expression
when I listened to music.

In Grandma May's generation she herself was "the
musical one." Her instrument was a tall golden harp like
the huge harps one sees on the stage at concerts in Carnegie
Hall. The harp stood, its gleaming brilliance modestly
shrouded in a fitted dust jacket, in the back parlor at
Deercreek.

Before I was four I sat on her lap while she played the
piano, now and then joining in, pounding on the keys in
mimicry of her long supple fingers. I learned to recognize
the common chord. At my request she would play it over
and over—a few chords leading up to it, then the one-
three-five, holding it a long time, letting it fill the room.

At last she taught it to me. I had to struggle to get
my fingers on the right keys—first, third, fifth. I often
went into that room alone to play the common chord. It
flooded me with happiness. It was as if I opened a door into
another world and that world was full of surprises and peace
and beauty.

This love of the common chord has stayed with me all
my life. I think it is an answer to prayer. It has healing
power. No wonder every hymn and anthem ends with it.

I remembered the names and sounds of all of grandmother's pieces. Finally she taught bits of them to me,
showed me the chords to play while she played a treble

part. Sometimes I sat beside her, just listening. As long as she would play I would listen. At my favorite parts I would laugh and she would look down at me, her smile indulgent, merry, quizzical.

Year by year I knew more of her pieces, waltzes and gallops and folk songs and hymns. There was one hymn that made me cry. At the end of it she would give a little sigh that was half groan, half a gasp—just a very small sound, but it would bring stinging hot tears to my eyes as if I had been struck.

The hymn was about a pilgrim, a stranger who could tarry but a night. And when my Grandma May sang it, so sadly, it was as if *she* was the pilgrim, *she* the stranger.

Children are well acquainted with grief. Infants come into the world weeping and it is only after a month or two of being mothered that they can smile. After that, grief recurs, but briefly, like a cloud going over the sun for a moment.

But in my grandmother's voice I heard a different grief, drawn up from a deep empty cavern.

I did not know why my grandmother's grief made my own heart ache so, but it did. At Deercreek, in the evenings, when the long portieres were drawn in front of the windows, the recesses behind them were like tiny secret rooms. Hidden away there in the dark, shut off from everyone, I would press my face against the cold glass of the windowpanes and cry, "Me too, Grandma May. I'm a pilgrim. I'm a stranger, too."

2

The Whipping

There are many different ways of remembering the past. One of the sharpest is the visual. Each of us has a photographic apparatus within us with which we can take pictures—just squeeze the bulb and the picture is taken.

Most houses have a photograph album on the living room table. At will a visitor can turn the pages, see the baby lying in a shell and laugh at the idea of its being the dignified master of the house.

We also have a mental album of images. We can look back and remember the incident, and see the picture. The puzzling thing is why one takes *that* picture and not another. Why not an amusing or attractive picture instead of one that is almost sinister?

For instance, there is one very fine photograph of Maynie, my lovely mother, that had a strong effect on my life. She is looking at me coldly. Unsmiling. Disapproving. Severe.

I remember I received a whipping for what I had done to deserve that look. A picture of the whipping—the little girl of five laid face down across her mother's lap, her skirts over her head, her drawers unbuttoned and let down while the bedroom slipper was vigorously applied to her bottom—would at least have been lively and dramatic, but there was no such picture in my album. Only this other—the awful look.

That look had the effect of making me feel myself to be a criminal on a large order. Bad people went to Hades, I knew, and I was bad because I never got enough sweets, never enough desserts, hard sauce, jam, maple syrup, and so I stole them. I was bad because I wanted my own way about everything and would fight to get it. That was being willful. And I would tell all the lies I needed.

This particular whipping was the result of my stealing chocolates and lying about it.

It happened on a Saturday. Reese had gone on an all-day boating excursion with his class. Mamma always did her shopping right after lunch. On this day she promised to take my sister Elma with her and drop her off at Mabel Webb's, her best friend. They would have the afternoon together. Bess, who was the baby, only a little more than two, was always put to bed for a long nap right after lunch. She would be asleep before Ellen, our nurse, had shut the door.

As I was five, I did not need to take a nap but I had to take a "rest." This meant lying down on the couch in the nursery, although I could read.

After lunch, before Mamma had got on her things to go out, she gave us each a chocolate, delicious little oblong blocks wrapped in jackets of silver foil.

She got them out of a box she took out of her clothes closet.

Elma asked me if I would give her my silver foil because she was making a ball of it.

Mamma was sitting down with Bess on her lap and she and Elma together were getting Bess's silver foil off and the chocolate in her mouth.

While they were fussing with Bess I looked for the place in the closet where Mamma kept the chocolates. I wanted another chocolate. Maybe two.

I waited until Mamma had gone, the house had quieted down and I was taking my rest on the nursery couch before going back to the closet to get the chocolates. I looked for the box. There it was. I dragged a chair across the room, put it in the closet, and climbed up on it. I took down the blue box and opened it; it was nearly full. Two would never be missed.

Picking out two, I moved the others about a little, and put the box back exactly where it had been. I took the chair back to Mamma's dressing table, and then very carefully removed the silver foil wrapped around the chocolates. That would be for Elma, for her ball of foil. How pleased and surprised she would be. Then I ate the chocolates, slowly, with great enjoyment.

Afterwards I began to think about the pieces of silver foil. It wouldn't be safe to give them to Elma. They might give everything away. I decided finally to keep them several days scrunched up in my flannel bag of jacks. Then I could bring them out as if I had found them outdoors.

I gave a last look around the room to be sure everything was in order—nothing disarranged on Mamma's dressing table, the chair where it always was, the door to the closet closed.

When Mamma returned I was seated on the floor in the nursery doing a picture puzzle. But my mother had no sooner entered her room than she called me.

I went to her in some alarm as her voice had been sharp. She was standing near the open door of her closet with the box of chocolates in her hand.

"Mary, you've been at these chocolates!"

"I have not!"

The lie was well told, not at all in a frightened voice; I was even a little indignant at the unjust accusation.

I looked right at her, and that must have been when I squeezed the bulb and took that photograph of her face—severe, unsmiling, disapproving. It went immediately into my mental album.

Those were the days when whippings followed crimes as a matter of course. When it was over and I stood sobbing, wiping my eyes and buttoning up my drawers, I could not help asking her, "But, Mamma, how did you find out?"

She pointed to the floor near her dressing table. There lay two tiny scraps of paper, the transparent paper that had interlined the silver foil jackets. I had not even noticed them.

There was nothing different about that whipping from a lot of others I had had, except that this one had been photographed, not the whipping but Mamma's face, to show how a mother felt when she had a bad girl for a daughter. The picture hung in my mental album, as clearly as if it hung on the wall before me.

A year later Mamma had to go to the hospital to have something cut out of her neck because it was pressing on her windpipe and choking her. Her thyroid gland had to be removed.

The operation was performed and word came from the hospital that it was successful and all danger now past. But later, bleeding began again and could not be stopped. With it, her life slowly ebbed away.

My understanding of death was as thin as that of the average six-year-old child. I could measure it only by the weeping. I saw that everyone was crying, even my Papa. He sat in his chair in the parlor with his white handkerchief in his hand, sobbing out loud and wiping his eyes. People from the church stood around, crying. The house servants stood in the hall, crying. Elma was kneeling before Papa, her face down on his knees. I knelt as close to her as I could get, trying to cry as hard as she was crying.

But nothing, of all this, made any change in that mental picture that hung in my album.

Mother was gone but the photograph was the same as ever: severe, frowning, unloving.

I lived with it as I grew up, through my years of marriage, motherhood and on past middle age, resignedly accepting the fact that my mother had never loved me.

I was sixty-seven before something happened to dispel that idea. It seemed almost a miracle. I was rummaging through a box sent to me as part of an inheritance. It was full of papers, mostly letters, and in the midst of these was a small manila notebook. On the title page was written "Baby Book of Baby May." In those days every young mother kept a baby book of each child's earliest words and deeds, up to the age of three or four.

I opened the book and saw, in my mother's own old-fashioned writing, her thoughts and reports about me. Why, she adored me! I was a pet. A beauty. So brilliant that I entertained everyone at Aunt Susie's big Christmas party.

But what was carried in my mind for all those years between—and there were sixty-two of them—was the look of severity, the disapproval, the unloving frown.

I've since had twenty-three years of her love and I've made the most of them. There is a picture of her sweet and smiling face by my bedside now. At the door of my bedroom, as one enters, are two of her watercolor sketches. One is a peaceful meadow scene at Deercreek. The other, a bit of sea whipping up into a storm. She was an accomplished artist.

3

Papa and I

I know that I was considered the most delicate of the four Alsop children, a fact I resented. I was passionately addicted to sports and envisioned myself as an athlete. I wanted to be right out there in front, competing on equal terms with the others.

When I was four I almost died of diphtheria. Following that, and in what seemed rapid succession, I succumbed to croup, mumps, measles, chicken pox, whooping cough, and lastly polio, which left me with curvature of the spine. I always had doctors looking out for me, first at Deercreek, and then at our home in Brooklyn.

As time went on I outgrew my disabilities and when my Papa, standing in the lower hall, shouted at the top of his lungs that he was going to do this or that and wanted a companion, it was likely to be me who joined him.

"I'm going to walk over the Brooklyn Bridge. Who wants to go?"

It gave me a sense of importance, and that is necessary for the third child in a family of four. Elma seemed to me the most important because she had already decided to live for others, and I could never do that. Besides, she was the eldest. And Reese was more important because he was a boy, and boys are more important than girls. Even Bess, three years younger than I, was more important because she was the "baby" and got all the indulgence and petting that the baby in the family always gets. As soon as she could talk, and was asked what her name was, she would say "Sweet Bess" and everyone thought this was unbearably cute.

Still, I knew I had a special standing with my Papa. He stood up for me whenever I was corrected and punished. Even, once, when I was expelled from school. Papa told Packer Institute, the private school I attended, "All my children are bright but Mary is the only genius."

Dr. Backus, the head of the school, replied, "Genius or not, Packer would be better off without her."

The problem was that I used the ten minutes allowed between classes to do my homework, walking very slowly down the corridors with my book open before me, concentrating fiercely on the page. I had a photographic memory, and gave fine recitations, often verbatim. The other girls tried to do the same but could not. I was a demoralizing influence.

Papa won me a reprieve.

Papa also had a special nickname for me, and it was the name of a state. None of the other children had anything like that.

On the July night I was born my parents were traveling through New Jersey to take up my father's new position as rector of St. Ann's in Brooklyn. I was, as it were, dropped en route. So I became "Jersey" to my father.

Papa and I liked to walk the bridge together. The Brooklyn Bridge was the first of the great suspension bridges that connect Brooklyn to Manhattan and Long Island. In later years, the Williamsburg and the Triborough were built, piercing the skies at different angles, different levels, like titans playing leapfrog over the city. But in those days when I came sliding down the banister to join my father, there was only the Brooklyn Bridge.

The Brooklyn Bridge began at Brooklyn City Hall, which was at the foot of our own Remsen Street. It arched across the river, the docks, the Battery and downtown New York and did not touch ground till it reached Wall Street.

Papa and I would walk to the exact middle of the bridge, where it seemed level, and would rest for a few minutes, watching the river traffic below, perhaps an ocean liner nosing its way slowly into a dock with fussy tugboats pulling and pushing at it.

My Papa was a crank about exercise: He did a daily dozen pushups every morning (we were expected to do the same), took a cold bath and the outdoor walk of two miles—one mile to the middle of the bridge, and one mile home.

I felt a great deal of pride when I walked with my father. I had heard someone say he had the head and profile of a Roman emperor. He certainly had the big nose.

The proper height for a man, I thought, was six feet. My father lacked two inches of that, being only five feet ten, but his carriage was lofty, and on Sundays and all formal occasions he wore a tall silk hat and an Inverness cape, and made, undeniably, a most impressive appearance.

For even a small child like myself, meeting him on the street, there would be a courtly bow and the sweeping off of the high hat. I felt this difficult to match with anything I had been taught in the way of a greeting.

When the ladies of his parish told him what a handsome appearance he presented standing in his white surplice before the congregation, he would whisper as if confiding a secret, "I can't help it!"

That was one of his stock remarks. I knew them all

and used to tease him about them. Another was, when he was presented with a new baby and expected to admire it, to exclaim, "Well, that *is* a baby!"

He was always impeccably groomed. His boots shone like mirrors. He had a special chair in his bathroom with a seat that lifted up, disclosing in the cavity, a boot-black's paraphernalia—pots of wax and polish, brushes and chamois skins. He never came down to breakfast and morning prayers without having first put that shine on his shoes.

There was a love of humor that ran through all Papa's talk. He quoted freely from other languages, but one never knew if it was authentic or a parody. He conjugated one Latin verb, *gormandizo, guzzleluare, snooziwi, flunktum.*

In a clergyman's family there are so few things to say when you are shocked. Not "My God!" for that would be taking the Lord's name in vain, and "Gosh," "Golly," and "Gee" are just abbreviations of the same. "By heaven" Papa disapproved of for it is God's dwelling place. Elma, who was interested in drama, swore by Shakespeare and we all got used to that though it was very funny as a cuss word. My father swore by his conscience. Very dignified.

On Sundays there came a time when my father could rest. Could actually close his eyes and take a nap in his study. I used to run ahead to help him arrange it.

He laid himself down on the couch; I folded his large black silk handkerchief, put it over his eyes, tucking the ends under his head. If he then remained motionless, I would tiptoe from the room. But if his arm lifted a little, I would creep in beside him and lay my head on his breast, his arm around me. We would nap together.

4

First Romance

My mother's journal records that when I was first born, my mother, after I had been oiled, bathed, dressed and laid beside her in the bed, told the nurse to bring in Reese, my brother, to see his new little sister.

Reese, blue-eyed and golden-haired, was thunderstruck. While my mother, smiling, explained who I was his eyes never left my face. At last he stretched out his hand, laid it upon me and announced firmly, "Dis *my* baby."

So began a romance that would last a lifetime. In a peculiar way I was his and he was mine in a unique relationship, similar to no other relationship I have known. Other people and long separations would not alter the way in which we had each other. We became practically one person, sharing everything.

My crib was put next to Reese's in our mother's bedroom, and she wrote in her journal how she was entertained in the early mornings and sometimes moved almost to tears by the sounds of us talking together. There were gurgles and squeals, little gasps of laughter. No doubt, communications of great importance.

When Bess was born it made no more difference to Reese than Elma, our older sister, did.

Reese was a gentler soul than I. When, a few years later, I would be locked into the spare room closet for punishment, he would stand at the door of the spare room and refuse to leave it so long as I was imprisoned. He would say over and over, "Baby May, p'ease be good; Baby May, p'ease be good."

Brooklyn Heights where we grew up was a select neighborhood with high-sounding names to its streets—Joralemon, Pierrepoint, Montague, Remsen, Clinton—but it was small in its extent, with very rough neighborhoods, even slums, all around. Sometimes slum children invaded us and we heard words and snatches of indecent songs of which we had no understanding.

When Reese was only eight, our father thought it best to acquaint him with what are called the facts of life, and Reese got the news to me immediately.

Our father, in making the explanation, did not bring the bees and pollen into it, as was at that time considered a useful method. He presented it as a mechanical process. But he was thorough and he was graphic, and Reese was the same when he explained it to me. Both of us thought it a surprising business but not more so than many grown-up goings-on, and if it was so, why that was all there was to it.

I had already known that Reese's body was much different from my own. I had found that out when we were just little naked children being undressed and bathed by our nurse and covered with towels and we would run about flicking the towels at each other.

As soon as we saw and understood that grown-up people went in pairs and called it being married, we decided that when we grew up we would marry each other and always be together. Then we learned that was not allowed if you were brother and sister. Reese came up with the idea that perhaps one of us had been adopted and when this was discovered we might get married after all. But it had not been discovered yet.

There were certain things we shared together. We loved ice skating. We would take our skates and go together on the trolley car to the St. Nicholas rink and skate. When we did something together we both loved, with that special sharing came something magical. The intensity of our happiness was indescribable. And we would look into each other's eyes and say, "We're here. We're here."

Another thing we shared was music, although Reese just sat beside me and listened while I played. I played by ear whatever song and dance tunes were popular, transposing them into my favorite key of F, but otherwise sticking to the arrangement of the composer. Then Reese would command, "Now play it big," and I would extemporize a concert arrangement with runs, arpeggios and lots of big crashing chords. Hours would pass that way.

When Reese was twelve he was sent away to boarding school, Groton, and we had each other only during the holidays. We were growing up. Now that we were so nearly grown, it was more important than ever that we should be alone together so that we could talk about life. But all day there were others around us and we were kept busy every minute. So he visited me at night.

My room was at the back of the house on the floor above his. The back wall was a bank of windows with a long window seat beneath. Reese would come up the long flight of stairs as silently as a shadow. We would each wrap ourselves in a downy and sit side by side on the window seat.

We talked for hours about ourselves and the lives that lay ahead of us. We were not rebels, we wanted to be good.

We wanted to live ideal lives, full of great experiences—the noblest, the most tender and the most beautiful.

We discussed the characters in the books we read. Many of them were not ideal at all. Virginity was demanded of girls but not of boys, and that was not fair. For each of us there would, of course, be one great, true love for which we would wait and remain virgin. Even the words that described virginity were beautiful—straight, pure, clean.

Sometimes we sat silent, dreaming about these concepts, our thoughts accompanied by the unceasing chorus of boat whistles that reached our windows from the bay. The waterways around Brooklyn were crowded with shipping. Ships came from all over the world and the eerie voices of the boats seemed to tell of those strange and faraway places, telling things we could not understand.

Some of the confidences we shared were very strange. Reese told me about a New Haven boardinghouse landlady who was showing a room to a boy who expected to go to Yale, and she said, "And I don't want to see no chippy's drawers hangin' on the gas jets."

We laughed, but we were shocked. Our eyes met and we thought the whole thing through.

Chippies went to boys' rooms and took off their drawers. Afterwards, the boys kept the drawers to brag about it. Hanging them on the gas jet was like hanging up a trophy.

None of this was ideal. Yet Reese was going to Yale when he was seventeen. Perhaps life was not ideal.

5

Prodigal

Children in my family were taught to pray as soon as we were big enough to kneel against the bars of our cribs, steeple our hands, bow our heads upon them and lisp, "God bless me." Later we received religious instruction both at home and at Sunday school.

In church, when the sermon began, we were under orders to listen and not daydream, and we would be examined on it at Sunday dinner which followed—a delectable feast, the culinary triumph of the whole week. If we remembered and could recite bits verbatim, we got some of the goodies, like salted almonds or marrons glacés.

After dinner each of us had to spend an hour alone in our rooms, reading the Bible and memorizing a few verses, and examining our consciences in order to discover our sins.

I knew already that I was vain. At every stage of my dressing and undressing, I admired my adolescent person and could see nothing wrong about it. To be an exhibitionist was a little worse and I was that too. I went to the Turkish baths when someone else was going, principally

31

because of the swimming pool afterwards. I would climb to the diving board, stretch up my arms and listen for the admiring remarks from the elephantine shapes clinging to the sides.

"Ain't she a lovely figure?"

Other sins were easy to find.

Avarice. You did not need to be old and wise to know that most of the crimes of history were committed because of a greed for money.

I knew I was extravagant. My dress allowance was not nearly enough, but that was only one thing. I wanted more of everything. Furs, clothes, jewels, riches, I wanted more and more. I wanted it all. I was insatiable.

I was not alone in my avarice—it was all around me, for standards of worldliness had to be maintained and that demanded money.

Eventually I overcame avarice, and freed myself from my cravings. But that was far, far in the future.

Every year I could understand more and more of the Bible, and some of the Old Testament stories were as good as anything in my fairy books.

The trouble was, you didn't know what to believe and what not to believe. I believed in their strange long names and memorized a lot of them—Nebuchadnezzar, Abednego, Meshach and Shadrach. You couldn't invent such names.

I believed God lived somewhere in the skies and sometimes talked to us in an ordinary voice, but no one could see who was speaking. I believed in the great hand that came down once and wrote a message on a wall. And I believed that when Daniel was thrown into the lions' den to be eaten by the lions, God pretended to be the lions' trainer and went into the den and stood beside Daniel so he was safe. But I didn't believe Jonah stayed three days, alive, in the whale's stomach. When I told my Sunday school teacher that, she said everything in the Bible was true.

I thought a great deal about God and I wanted to know what he looked like, but could not accept the old man with a long white beard nor even the Bible's description—the hair of white wool and brass feet. My own picture was a half-seen figure wrapped in a cloak and made even more mysterious because a sort of small whirlwind shimmered around him. But inside all this movement was a shape like our human shape. And from it poured a flood of something—I could almost feel it reach me—like a beam of sunshine on a cold day. It bound us together. He had something to do with me. Something good. They said he was our heavenly father, that he had made us and the whole universe and was almighty and in charge of everything. It was to him I had been praying all these years.

I had studied my catechism and knew the creed by heart, also my duty to God and my duty to my neighbor.

But now I was fourteen and had an active and logical mind.

One day I noticed what I was actually saying when I said the creed. "I believe in God the father almighty, maker of Heaven and earth."

So much was all right. What came next was all wrong. "And in Jesus Christ, his only son, our Lord," as if Jesus was a special child. Why, that gave God a family like father's, with a wife and children.

To say the creed once a week in church was not enough for my papa. We said it every day at morning prayers. When the breakfast bell had rung, everyone assembled in the dining room, and took their places at the big oblong table, each standing behind his own chair. The first thing we did was the singing of the doxology. I was given the nod by father and sang one clear note, F above middle C, and they all joined in and sang it in unison.

Next, everyone recited the creed.

But one day there was a hitch in the performance. I had begun to think. Not only to think but to listen and hear each word and the extraordinary sentences they added up to. So heard and considered, it was as fantastic a tale and as unbelievable as anything in *Grimm's Fairy Tales*.

When next the creed was said, I kept my lips closed. Father noticed but said nothing.

The same thing happened on the second day. On the third day father interrupted the recital.

"Mary, you are not saying the creed."

I answered, "I can't say it, Papa, I don't believe it."

Papa was not harsh with me about this. He came to my room a few days later with an armful of books telling me that these theological works held the answer to my doubts, quoting the German poet Schiller, who wrote, *Der hat nie gezweifelt, der hat nie geglaubt* ("He who has never doubted, has never believed").

Smiling, he talked about the biblical parable of the Prodigal Son, only this would be the Prodigal Daughter. He even made a joke about it. "How's the Prod this morning?"

Soon everyone in the church knew all about it, and a girl in my Sunday school class asked me if it was true I was an atheist. She looked almost frightened.

Atheist! Unbeliever! Denyer of God! Me! an atheist! I, who prayed all the time! I, who held long conversations with Him, marveling at his closeness, at the way he gave me what I asked for, even a silly thing like beating Lottie Blair in a spelling match, or a nice sunny day for the picnic, or in winter, a little beaver muff with a small purse built in.

I never forgot my manners with Him.

"Thanks ever so much, God," I would conclude my prayers.

There was an anthem they sang in church, the Te Deum, for people who could not think up their own words of thanks. Dozens of choir boys and men standing in their

white surplices, roared, "All the earth doth worship thee/
The father everlasting."

I could make nothing of the theological doctrines of
the Trinity, of the Incarnation, of the Redemption and
salvation—in other words, the creed—but I could love God
and thank him.

Nobody expects to understand God. That would be
absurd, as if the smaller could encompass the larger. But
we can turn our faces toward His sun and warmth, and we
can lift up our gates that the King of Glory can come in.

When Papa asked me if I intended to go to church
regularly from now on, I said not regularly but sometimes.
It made him angry, but eventually we stopped arguing.

It was later that same year that I read a book called
Martin Eden by Jack London. I had read other books by him
but nothing like this. When I read those two words he
used—the *cosmic sadness*—my heart missed a beat. It felt as
if a message had been sent to me from a far distant land,
encircling the world and accompanied by a sound, the
sound of sadness, and a color, the color of sadness, and the
touch that lays its hand on everything that is mortal.

I had always known sadness; my heart had often ached
with a mysterious sense of loss, a curious feeling of misfit.
Now that I knew it was cosmic I made it my own. I
incorporated the words into my vocabulary.

Unhappy? Depressed? It was the cosmic sadness.

6

Melusina

My Aunt Mellie was not at
all like my mother. Although they were both almost
beauties, and both had inherited the splendid teeth of their
mother, her regular features and air of distinction, the
similarities stopped there. Their enmity was more than the
usual sibling rivalry.

Maynie, my mother, was famous for her sweetness and
charm. She was the favorite of the whole big Denny family.
Mellie was famous for her rages. If she was opposed, or did
not get what she wanted, her voice rose and suddenly she
was possessed by an uncontrollable fury. Everyone hastened
to give her what she wanted, do her will, quiet her down.
Only one person could control her—my grandmother, her
mother. Aunt Mellie worshiped her mother.

Once at Deercreek when I was four years old, I came
around a corner of the house and suddenly stopped because
I saw my mother and my aunt standing about six feet apart,
motionless, staring at each other. Suddenly Aunty stepped
forward and struck Mamma in the face.

I had seen children fight, and cats and dogs, but never

grown ladies. I turned and ran back to the kitchen porch where Lili, my nurse, was seated, doing her mending. Marietta, the housemaid, was there too. I told them what I had seen.

"Don't say such things, Baby May. That's a naughty girl."

"Yes, I did! I did too! I saw her!"

They explained to me at length how they knew that such a thing could not have happened because such things never happened. But though I tried to be a good girl and unsee what I had seen, I was never able to. Aunty hit my mother in the face.

Whatever Maynie had and prized, small or large, a flower, a garment, a service rendered by one of the maids, Aunty envied and took away from her. Mellie had never married. Looking back over the years, I can see that what Aunty envied our mother for the most was us children. Four little ones to own, possess utterly, guide, mould, shape according to her will.

Aunty competed with mother for our allegiance, asserting authority over us, nursing us through our illnesses.

At the time our mother died, Grandma May and Aunty were in Germany. Grandma May immediately wired my father to send the girls over to her. Papa closed the rectory and took Reese to live with him at a hotel.

Grandma May's entire entourage was with her. She never traveled without a few companions, usually the daughters of indigent noble families, who could be useful or at least entertaining to her.

The new arrangement placed us, of course, under the immediate supervision of Aunty.

Aunty had once been engaged but broke it off. People said it was because he was a strong man and she knew she could not have dominated him. She now accepted the charge of the three of us as a solemn duty to her dead sister, renouncing all thought of husband and children of her own, promising to be a second mother to us.

Elma was ten years old when our mother died, and so resented the idea that any one could replace mother that she turned against Aunty with a resentment which she never got over.

I was only six, and Aunty took complete possession of me. As if to balance her rages, Aunty had a bewitching way with her when she wanted to fascinate anyone. She could first terrify me, then twist me around her little finger.

Elma, Bess, and I stayed with Grandma May and Aunty for about two years—two years of aimless wandering, going from one hotel to another. Aunty put into effect her very strict ideas as to how girls should be brought up.

To say that Aunty was thorough in her dealings with us would hardly begin to suggest the lengths to which she went, telling us what we must do, wear, eat, read, whom we should see, how long and what instrument we must practice—all was laid out for us.

As the musical one, I was started on the violin, which I hated because of the squeaks. I loved the piano because on it I could improvise and harmonize.

Once I transgressed Aunty's rules by playing the hotel piano—very softly with the soft pedal down, harmonizing "Swanee River"—when I should have been practicing the violin. Aunty caught me.

She swept me off the piano stool and sent me spinning to the floor. As I picked myself up she grabbed me by the back of the neck and, to my shame and embarrassment, marched me through the public rooms of the hotel in the direction of our own suite.

I made several breaks for freedom but her iron fingers bit strongly into my neck. I assumed a jaunty, half-smiling air, hoping to avoid the appearance of one being led to the guillotine.

Arriving in our own rooms, she sat down and forced

me to stand in front of her and recite the full and detailed
story of my disobedience.

Afterwards she tried to win me back. An expression of
deepest sorrow shadowed her face. Her head on one side,
she grieved over me, trying to smile through her tears,
murmuring, "Oh, my little Madchen! My little Madchen!"
I broke down and cried with her, and she forgave me.
She wiped her eyes and mine, cheered me up, talked about
how I had always been peculiarly her own, how she had
understood me better than my mother.

She then took me out to lunch and introduced me to
gourmet food—raw oysters on the half shell.

We came back to the United States when Grandma
May bought a house in Brooklyn. It was big enough for
both families, Grandma May and Aunty and all their
attendants, and father and his four motherless children.
This uniting of the two families returned us to the same
streets and scenes and neighbors we had known all our
lives.

A big upstairs room that was the full width of the
house became our playroom. In it were boxes of toys,
books, tools, and a horrible instrument called a clavier
which looked like a piano. It was guaranteed to produce a
superior technique in record time because it gave out no
musical tones, only clicks; several violins, guitars, banjos,
mandolins, and a queer thing shaped like a potato with
holes along one side which gave forth a hollow moaning
sound. I was particularly addicted to this.

I became quite an accomplished violinist. I took
lessons from the tall gray-bearded Herr Shradieck, and
struggled to master the instrument well enough so that
there would not be one horrible squeak to make my blood
run cold. One day he stopped me playing and talked to me
seriously about becoming a professional virtuoso, assuring
me that I could become famous. But I had no desire to be

famous. I played at recitals because Aunty made me.

My fear of Aunty had grown deeper. It was fear mixed with horror, for I had become aware of her duplicity, the way she would turn on her charm, be sweet, win me over till I yielded up my secrets, my hiding places, even made confessions of sins not yet discovered. Then, *wham!*

She had a hold on me that was almost hypnotic, like a snake fixing a bird with its eye—and I was helpless.

She wore a cluster of thin gold bangles on her arm that tinkled as she walked, announcing, *I am coming, I am coming.* The mere sound of them in the hall made my heart leap and pound, and sometimes I could see the demon in her eyes.

7

Matrigna

One day Aunty proposed to Papa that she and Grandma May take us to Europe again. Papa protested that it would interfere with our schooling. There ensued the first of many arguments, but Papa finally gave in when Aunty promised it would only be for a few months.

The promise was never kept. The trip turned into a dramatic flight, punctuated by periodic alarms when envoys sent by Papa seemed about to intercept us. At one point, Grandma May, feeling keenly each broken promise to have us returned to our father, cabled, over Aunty's protests, that it should be done.

Aunty fought bitterly over the plan to have us returned, working herself up to a pitch that frightened us all. Grandma May sat quietly in her armchair while Aunty walked up and down the long salon of our hotel suite, wringing her hands and crying "No, no, Maman! You can't! You can't!"

I was so shocked that I forgot she was my enemy and

ran to her and threw my arms around her waist. She pushed me away.

"Mellie, control yourself," Grandma May said. "You're hysterical."

But Aunty screamed so that Grandma May told our friend Signorina, "Get the doctor to come immediately, Thierry. She'll make herself ill." And Signorina hurried away to obey, while the maid got out some smelling salts and followed Aunty holding the bottle to her face.

Aunty ran to the window.

Our suite was on the eighth floor. In a moment, Aunty had lifted the lower sash and thrown one leg over the broad sill. Elma and Fraulein held on to her desperately but she beat them off. She was most of the way out of the window, her head down on the sill, when Grandma May capitulated.

"All right! Mellie, stop! I'll do whatever you want!"

Her face was ashen white.

Thierry came with the doctor. Aunty was taken to her room and put to bed and given a bromide. Doctor's orders were to do nothing that might upset her.

Papa, realizing at last that Aunty was going to do exactly as she pleased and that he was powerless to prevent her, philosophically resigned himself to the fact.

Our odyssey lasted two years and ended at last when we came to the sands of the Sahara.

Our father, deprived of his daughters, had not languished in loneliness; he had remarried. Elma was outraged that Papa should have got married again and put another woman in our dear mother's place. She held it against Matrigna, Papa's new wife, and never got over that feeling.

Papa and Matrigna had left Brooklyn and were already at the seaside resort where we would spend the summer when we arrived in New York on our return from the Sahara.

The resort was Digby, Nova Scotia, on the Bay of Fundy, where there was sailing, fishing, swimming. Digby was a quaint village divided evenly between summer people and "natives." Old farmhouses were enlarged and re-modeled to feed and shelter summer guests. There were cottages to rent or buy, a golf course and tennis courts. It had become popular and exclusive. The right people liked to summer there. Elma and I, upon returning to the United States, were sent off to join them there.

Before letting us go, Aunty perpetrated one last atrocity. She removed from our luggage every attractive or even decent coat, hat, and blouse that we had. Where she got the rags she substituted for them, I have no idea. I had never seen such clothes. So attired, we had to go to Digby and meet our new stepmother. As it was an important and exciting occasion, we were ashamed.

I liked Matrigna at first sight. A maiden lady, near middle age, her real name was Righter, of a substantial, well-known and well-connected family of Newark, New Jersey. We decided to call her Matrigna, which is the Italian word for stepmother, as soon as Papa wrote us about her. Fortunately she liked it.

Matrigna was tall, a little overweight, with lots of brown hair done without any style or cleverness, and her face was full and pink. But she held herself well, and showed character and authority in the way her vivid blue eyes met yours so directly.

This second marriage of Papa's was a great success. It was a love marriage as his first had been. Matrigna adored him, ran his house well, managed the servants and was faithfully his better half as long as he lived.

Almost the first thing she had to do when we reached Digby was take us to St. John and buy us decent clothes. She seemed to enjoy it. We had never had such clothes. They were conventional and what is called smart. Aunty had always designed our clothes herself—they were what she called artistic, made of very rich materials.

As I was fourteen, an age when most girls still needed a mother's guidance, Matrigna took me especially under her wing and arranged little parties for me to meet and become friends with those of my own age whom it would be nice for me to know.

As the summer went on, parties multiplied: sailing parties, moonlight rides in a big hay rick, tennis tournaments. Little dancing parties with just half a dozen couples. I saw, with much interest and pleasure, that everyone was flirting quite as if we had all been of marriageable age. We began to pair off. The older people knew who was "going with" whom and they were placed beside each other at dinner parties and always included as a couple.

I acquired a heavy suitor. He was a young lawyer ten years older than I who was spending his vacation with his parents at Digby. Matrigna, pleased at my conquest, told me he was "quite a catch."

There was no doubt I was going to have to say yes or no to marriage before the summer ended. Though I was young for such a decision, I had definite convictions: my husband-to-be must be just the right man for me. And this was not he. Sadly, I refused him.

No other suitors clamored for my hand, but I got plenty of attention, though I was considered a bit too shy and reserved. All things considered, I had the best time that summer I had ever had in my life. No more continual pressures to study, work, learn languages, practice. And I was free from Aunty.

In September we returned to Brooklyn and I resumed my regular schooling at Packer. Elma went to Philadelphia to enter the Woman's Medical College. Bessie, now eleven, would live with Grandma May.

When young people inherit fortunes it is customary that a trustee remains in power over the holdings for a number of years to prevent unwise spending. When we discovered we were to inherit some money from Grandma May, we were not surprised to find that we had a trustee, but profoundly displeased that the trustee was Aunty. However, Grandma May, as if to protect us from her own daughter, had stipulated in her will that each of us, on coming of age, should receive an allowance of twenty-four hundred dollars a year.

At the time, if a young person spent a year or two away from home at a finishing school, that was considered a good way to meet young people from other cities. It had to be, of course, the right school, such as Farmington or Briarcliffe, or Dobbs Ferry or Ingleside.

Matrigna was an old Farmington girl herself, but I decided that Ingleside had more sports and athletics.

I went to Ingleside for two years. After Ingleside I had a coming-out party. (I had heard of girls "leaking" out— just beginning to do more and more socially, but Matrigna insisted that I be one of the regular debutantes of 1903.)

For several years past I had been getting a great deal of attention from boys. (If they were of college age, we called them men.) One of these, Henry Vandenburg, a Harvard junior, had been proposing to me frequently. One day, considerably to my own surprise, I heard myself saying yes to him. We had been playing our banjos together. We both loved music.

He was of course tall and good-looking. (I wouldn't look at anyone who wasn't.) What I remember most clearly about his face was the sweetness of his smile. It was never a broad smile, it barely parted his lips but the sweetness lingered when the smile was ended.

Almost immediately I realized I had been insincere, that I wanted Henry for a dancing partner, an escort, a suitor always at my beck and call, but that was all. And at the first opportunity I explained to him that it was just sort of a game—flirting—not binding on either of us.

I did not really care for him that way and it would not have been fair to let him think so.

But Henry persisted. He replied that he *did* care for me and always would. So he remained engaged to me whether I was engaged to him or not. Girls sometimes changed their minds, he reasoned. If, meanwhile, I would just keep on letting him be the one with whom I danced the cotillions and went out with more than anyone else, he would be grateful for that now and just bide his time and wait.

Both our families approved and made opportunities for us to be together.

8

Motorcar

On our block the houses adjoined one another, presenting an unbroken façade to the street. They were four or five stories high, in addition to a basement which was considerably lower than the street, with a small paved area in front where deliveries could be made.

In those days we had plenty of servants. They had their sleeping quarters on the fourth floor, under the roof. For daytime use they had the whole basement to themselves, as well as a big living room at the front of the house, and the laundry and kitchen.

On the second floor a large spare room was at the front, the master bedroom in the middle, and the family sitting room at the back. A small hall bedroom was directly over the entrance hall.

We three girls had the third floor to ourselves. Reese was usually away at boarding school or college so he had the hall bedroom on the second floor.

One day, while we were all in the upstairs sitting room, my father made an announcement. Papa had received a letter from a distant cousin whom he had known quite well when he was young and living in Philadelphia. Her last name had been Kane, a fine old Philadelphia family, going back to the famous Arctic explorer Elisha Kent Kane. The women of the family were famous for their beauty.

"I remember her quite well," father told us. "Her name was Georgette. She got married in St. Steven's Church when I was a curate there."

The man she married was a Bostonian named William Parrot, a French name, pronounced not like the bird, but with a silent "t." She was now living in Arizona but one of her children, the youngest boy, had taken a job in New York and would like to come over to Brooklyn to visit us. The question was, which one of us girls must go down and receive and entertain our expected guest.

Papa did some figuring and decided he must be about sixteen.

Then, of course, it would be Bess.

The Philadelphia cousin arrived on a Sunday. Bess went down to do her duty. He did not stay long. When Bess returned, her face was bright with interest.

"He's not a boy, he's a man. He's twenty-four years old. He's very handsome and taller than Reese. And he came in a motocar across the Brooklyn Bridge."

There were generally three ways to get from Brooklyn to New York. By coach or buggy—by far the most elegant way, but also the way that took the most time, and besides, few people had horses. By ferry, which was both short and cheap, but which docked at the waterfront near the Battery, leaving a long way to go to reach the shops and theaters. And by subway—the most convenient way of all. It went under the river and most of New York (which people were now beginning to call Manhattan), with stops all along the way from Wall Street to Carnegie Hall.

I had once, as the guest of wealthy friends of my father's, crossed the bridge in a luxurious private brougham with an Irish coachman holding the reins over a beautiful pair of grays. We had driven to the very door of the Metropolitan Opera House, where I heard Caruso sing *Rigoletto*.

But a motorcar was a rarity. I had seen them, of course, but I had never been in one. Our newfound cousin's motorcar made a distinct impression.

The young man called again. This time Papa and Matrigna were at home and we all met him. I rather disliked him. After a little social chatting Papa, Matrigna, and I withdrew, leaving Bess to entertain him.

He continued visiting, and although I kept palming him off on Bess, when he telephoned it was usually I who answered and we would have a telephone visit with a little bantering and laughter. At last he asked me if I would go out with him in his car—to Coney Island or wherever I would like.

I had been ready to resist him when I went to answer the telephone, but his words had acted like magic, and I heard myself saying with alacrity that that would be delightful.

Getting acquainted is a mysterious business involving, of necessity, the asking and answering of many questions.

Kent Parrot and I were third cousins. He was the last of ten children. When it came to naming him, his parents, in desperation, had named him Elisha Kent Kane, in honor of the Arctic explorer. Of course he had dropped Elisha.

He told me of the brutal bullying he had received at the hands of his elder brothers, being the littlest and youngest. The appalling practical jokes. The terror-ridden nights.

"They all but murdered me," he said. "But I grew up fast, and taller than any of them. Then I could give it as well as take it."

As he finished speaking, there was an ugly downward twist at the corner of his mouth. It made him look jeering. Cynical.

As summer began, it was understood now, and accepted, that I was the one the new cousin came to see. I would be sitting there on the flight of steps leading from street to stoop, a step lower than anyone else, with my coat over my arm, when Kent's motorcar would drive up and stop at the curb.

I no longer disliked him. I felt, instead, a little pride, as the tall young man came slowly up the steps, greeting the family, stopping beside me.

On our rides Kent was wholly intent upon me and not at all in the same way other men had been. His mere presence beside me was a disturbing force that made me feel helpless and inadequate.

I wondered if he had really fallen for me or was just giving me a rush. Or if I had fallen for him. I certainly admired his superb physique—broad-shouldered, narrow-hipped, and long-limbed. He had a fine head with very thick dark hair. He carried his head a little to one side and for some reason or other that gave an impression of irresistible determination. From under that tilt of his head his eyes looked out without expression, blue, unwavering and cold.

Somehow I had a sense of his being important. He wasn't really. But I was sure that if he was in a crowded room everyone would notice him. They would take a second glance, then stare and wonder who he could be that he was so certain in advance he would always get exactly what he wanted.

I said to myself, if it is me he wants, His Highness may find himself mistaken. But there was no doubt he frightened me a little. I decided the best thing would be not to go out with him again. I refused his next invitation. And the next. When Kent called again there had been a change of weather from a windy dryness, which had made me nervous, to a balmy and moist seductiveness that made the whole world seem open and fragrant. I longed to float out into it. I accepted.

On this occasion he asked, "Wouldn't you like to drive? I think you'd enjoy it. I'll show you how."

I had always loved to drive my grandmother's horses at Deercreek, whispering, "Go faster, John." (I always managed to get the seat beside the driver.) And when, during our summer vacations at Digby or Sunapee Lake, the most delightful attention young gentlemen could pay me would be to take me out driving in a buggy with one horse, or a runabout with two horses.

But to drive a motorcar!

Kent waited till we came to a wide road empty of traffic and stopped the car, gave me a few directions, helped me with a few starts and stops, then left it to me. An hour later, when he took over again he said casually, "You're a winner at the wheel." After that I went out quite often with him.

Then Kent began to talk about the Maine woods. He and his brothers were expert woodsmen, able to live in the woods like Indians, on fish and game. In winter, when the lakes were frozen, they'd get moose and elk. In summer they traveled by canoe, making a portage between one lake and the next, carrying the canoes around the worst falls then launching them again where the stream was navigable.

I listened, enthralled. It was exactly the sort of life I loved. I read books about it with delight.

"I could show you a stream," he said, "where, if you throw your line into it with half a dozen flies on the leader, the water will simply boil with leaping trout, rainbow trout."

I still felt that slight fear of him, perhaps because I couldn't understand him, but I was getting used to it. And I was sure now that he was not just giving me a rush. He was still intent upon me like an arrow once aimed and then never swerving.

Well, what was I going to do about it? Could I do anything?

He never tried to touch me, not even his arm around

me getting in or out of the car or his hand over mine on the wheel. No long pleading looks into my eyes.

As we neared home one evening, he was driving and still talking about the Maine woods. He pulled up the car before we reached the house.

"That's where we'll take our honeymoon. In the Maine woods," he said.

Automatically I reached for safety—I brought up my engagement to Henry. "I'm engaged to someone else."

His answer came instantly and without the slightest change of expression.

"You can break it."

He started the car again, drove it the short distance to the house and stopped. All the lights in the house were out except the downstairs hall lights, kept on, of course, for me. It must have been late. As we went up the steps I was trying to gather my wits. I was not going to agree to this. There was a big "No" within me ready to burst out, but something prevented my speaking, and when we reached the top, I still said nothing.

Kent touched the door bell. I knew Minnie would be waiting to let me in.

"I'll call you tomorrow," Kent said as the door opened. He ran down the steps and I went in.

I still had that "No" pent up within me. I had come too close to a stream with a dangerously strong current and I had been caught into it. I had made no decision, but a decision had been made and it was now quite far behind me, and I was in a new world, committed to it. I felt different within myself. I had a new identity.

The next day my father said to Elma, "I don't know what's happened to Mary. She walks around the house like someone in a trance."

And Elma said, "Why, Papa, she's engaged! She's going to marry Kent Parrot!"

9

Rats

Though I am so far removed from it all now, I remember quite clearly the disturbance it created in the house when Elma announced that I was going to marry Kent. But the statement did not go unchallenged. Elma was given to exaggeration and Papa simply did not believe her.

"Nonsense, Elma. Don't exaggerate! She's just having a fling with a new beau! Or maybe a motorcar!" His joke tickled him.

But when, within twenty-four hours, Mr. Barr, one of the vestrymen at St. Ann's, stopped Papa on the street and said jovially, "What's this I hear? Mary engaged? And who's the distant cousin?" Papa felt something would have to be done.

That night I heard his firm tread on the stairs. "Yo-ho, I'm coming up!"

My door usually stood open but it was shut today because I had a secret to hug to myself. Of course it was not quite a secret anymore. I had told Ethel, my best friend, and when she pleaded to be allowed to tell Adelaid, her

53

next best friend, I had given permission, but only to tell Adelaid. Adelaid, however, was under no restrictions except the usual "Don't tell anybody," which really meant the reverse.

I felt guilty because I had not had the necessary talk with Papa first and I knew I was going to get it. I ran to open the door.

Papa was in a good humor. He wouldn't come in, but just stood in the doorway.

"I haven't come to scold you, my dear, but to help you out of a jam. You're being talked about."

"Who's talking about me?"

"Mr. Barr. Came up to me on the street and said he'd heard you were engaged to this Parrot fellow. You'll have to stop going out with him, at least for a while. Perhaps you can see him next fall again when we come back from Sunapee Lake, if you enjoy the rides so much."

"What did you say to Mr. Barr?"

"I simply denied it."

"But, Papa, it's true."

He frowned, puzzled. "*What* is true?"

"Well—Kent and I are engaged."

He said angrily, "Don't say such silly things. How can you be engaged without my knowing anything about it?"

"Well—I was getting ready to tell you."

"In any case, it's out of the question. I shouldn't think of allowing it."

"Papa, you can't say that. Maybe you don't like him now. I admit he's kind of hard to get used to. But you will." I spoke coaxingly.

It is my belief that he had never really *seen* his cousin before. Now, in his mind's eye, my father looked at Kent and truly *saw* him, and detested him with a violent detestation that was to last as long as he lived.

"You must have seen it coming," I added.

"I did not," he said emphatically, "and I'm sorry

you've got so involved, for you can't possibly marry him."

"Why not?"

"Because he's not fit to be your husband."

I was angry now too. "How can you say such a thing? You don't know him. You haven't even talked to him."

"I don't have to. I've seen him. And I've seen his mother."

"His mother? What's *she* got to do with it?"

"It's my opinion she was—well—fast."

"Oh, rats!"

At this nasty bit of filial rudeness my Papa lost his temper. "Don't be vulgar!" he shouted. "Don't be cheap and common!" With this he stamped from the room.

I had damaged my cause and regretted it but could not help feeling that the situation would yield to reason, or time, or something. Just let it simmer. Meanwhile where could I meet Kent? It would be most unpleasant for him to come here. So, via the subway, I went to New York and met him for lunch at the Waldorf.

As a general thing I conformed to house rules, one of which was, when you are going out always tell someone where you are going. So I told Matrigna that I was going to the Waldorf to lunch with Kent. I half suspected that she liked Kent a little, though of course she had to side with Papa. She shook her head sadly, looking at me reproachfully.

Elma had been on my side from the beginning. You hear a lot nowadays about sibling rivalry. As children we had quarreled and fought violently, for the fun of it. It was one of our best sports, to tangle in a clump on the nursery floor and fight furiously without making a sound, so that we would not be interrupted and our fun cut short. But now that we were grown we closed ranks and helped each other.

Elma had already promised to give me my entire trousseau. She loved clothes as much as I did. And we had

already been to Loeser's together looking at hand-embroi-
dered underwear, and chose some lovely things and brought
them home to gloat over.

I lunched in New York with Kent several times and
noticed what I had already surmised—among strangers he
stood out. The moment we entered and the headwaiter
caught sight of us we got the best table available.

At one of these lunches Kent told me about his
feldspar. Even after he got through explaining what it was,
I couldn't visualize it clearly. It's in the ground but not an
ore like gold or silver, a sort of asphalt and very valuable.
He had found some off in the woods. "Extensive outcrop-
pings" he had said, and when I asked what that meant he
replied, "It means riches! Money rolling in!"

"Really riches, Kent?"

Kent gave his sudden loud laugh. "Riches enough to
give you everything your little heart desires. What would
you like? A tiara? A string of pearls?"

I was elated but not surprised. That's what one would
expect from a man like Kent. "I'll make a list!" I cried. "I
rather prefer emeralds."

"Then emeralds it will be," he said, quite calm and
serious now.

He was not bluffing. He had complete confidence in
himself. I never saw a shred of doubt in him.

My father came to see me again, this time evidently
prepared for a longer talk. He took my one easy chair and
turned it to face me.

"In our last talk," he began in a matter-of-fact voice,
"you said I did not know and had not talked with Mr.
Parrot, implying that I was judging him before I had
examined him. There is some justice in your accusation. So
I telephoned him."

"When?"

"Yesterday. A woman answered. She had a very
common voice."

"That's his landlady. He lives at a boardinghouse."

"So I gathered. She said he was probably at the garage and gave me that number."

"He's there a lot," I said. "He's a gas-engine consultant." It sounded very grand to me.

"Gas-engine consultant," repeated my father thoughtfully. "Well. Maybe. He told me he bought and sold used cars."

"It's all the same. You do both," I explained.

My father continued. "I got him at the garage and asked him a few questions. I must say, trying to get a straight answer out of that young man is like pulling teeth."

"What did you ask him?"

"What any father would ask. I wanted some character references. Names and addresses of people who could vouch for him."

"And what did he say?"

"Had none to give me. Had only been living here a short while. All his relatives and friends were in or near Boston."

After a short but significant pause, Papa continued. "McConnell has a brother who is the vice-president of a bank in Boston. I've talked with him already. He knows all about the Parrots. They are notorious."

McConnell was rector of Trinity Church. I had known him all my life. Dr. David McConnell was my father's best friend and had been one of Bess's godparents.

"Notorious," I repeated. My lips felt dry. "How notorious?"

"Those young men, I suppose this fellow's brothers, are not much better than a gang of thugs. The Pro boys—that's what the police called them."

"The police!"

"Oh, yes, the police. They were watched by the police of two states. Massachusetts and Maine. Once they helped themselves to a locomotive from a railroad yard and crossed the state with it."

I laughed. "But, Papa, that's a prank. That's just crazy kids doing crazy things for the fun of it."

"It got them locked up."

"They never put them in jail for a thing like that!"

"Well, yes. But they got out. No one knows how. The whole thing is, they had no upbringing. Their father had asthma very badly and he and his wife were away, hunting for a climate that would alleviate it. They paid no attention to their children—whether they were in school or out."

My father's voice came to a stop and I said nothing, feeling that, really, there was nothing very serious against Kent in all he had said.

Papa stood up, ready to go. At the door he paused and said, "I don't like to invite or give heed to gossip, but in this case it's my duty. Moreover, where there's so much smoke there must be some fire. I'll know when I talk to him."

"You're going to see him?"

"Certainly. Deal with him face to face."

"When?"

"Tomorrow at five. And I must ask you, as I've already asked your Matrigna, to keep out of this. I must be alone with him. This is not a social occasion."

When the time came I found it very difficult to comply. I went out in the hall and stood on the stairs, listening to my father's voice, and the occasional monosyllables from Kent.

At last I could stand it no longer. I went all the way downstairs and walked along the hall from front to back, glancing in at the parlor as I passed the door.

The scene before me was not reassuring. They faced each other, quite far apart, Papa on the sofa with a notebook and pencil in hand, his eagerness apparent in the forward tilt of his body and his whole attitude. Kent was expressionless and slightly sullen, lounging back comfortably in his chair in a way that was, somehow, insulting.

As I passed the door I heard my father say, "And have you any means of support besides the used-car business?"

I could hardly hear Kent's answer, it was not much more than a grunt, but I thought it was yes. And I wondered if he meant the feldspar. Then I simply could not stand it any longer so I went into the parlor. Neither of them paid the slightest attention to me. I sat down, not very near them.

Papa asked, "And what was your college?"

"Dartmouth."

"What year?" Papa wrote in his notebook.

"I didn't finish."

"Why not?" Papa waited a long time for the answer, his pencil poised. The answer never did come.

Kent just stared at him, almost absentmindedly.

At last Papa understood he was not going to be answered and wrote something quite lengthy in his notebook, then put it away and stood up. Kent and I stood up as well. I was so furious at the cruel grilling Kent was getting that I was crying. I was trying to conceal it but my face was all crumpled up.

Papa said, "Well, Mr. Parrot, that'll do for today, I think." But Kent was looking at me.

I couldn't help a strangled sob.

Papa looked from me to Kent then back to me several times. He then marched out of the room and up the stairs. I flung myself at Kent. He sat down again, took me on his lap, wrapped his arms around me and held me close. I put my face in his neck and bawled.

10

Marriage

During the summer, those whose work did not keep them in the cities fled to the country to escape the sweltering heat. Only the less fortunate remained. Asphalt roads were so softened by the sun that pedestrians' shoes sank into them. Mountain resorts, lake resorts, ocean beaches did a thriving business.

Clergymen, rectors of big-city parishes, were among the lucky ones who could get away. The exodus would begin in mid-June, when school closed. This year, 1905, we were going to Sunapee Lake, New Hampshire, one of our favorite vacation spots. We had rented a lakeside cottage with a tennis court long ago.

Matrigna liked Sunapee because it relieved her of housekeeping. We would all take our meals at a neighboring farmhouse where they set a very good table. A completely satisfactory outlook except for my defiance of my father.

The summer was like nothing I had ever experienced before. Heretofore the world, for me, had been my own little environment, my house, my room, my own self. Now its boundaries had exploded for me. It was immense. It spread out on all sides of me and I found myself immersed it it.

I was bursting with love, not only for Kent but for the whole world and all the people in it, as if it was all a part of me. This strange feeling was so overwhelming that the practical matters of my marriage were forgotten. That Papa opposed us was a trifle. Something would change that, because I was a different person. It was a *fait accompli*.

I realized, however, that sooner or later plans would have to be made. Papa showed no signs of giving in, so a church wedding at St. Ann's was out of the question. There was always, as a last resort, an elopement with a civil ceremony at city hall. I did not want that. It seemed cheap and shady. Another possibility was a house wedding, the clergyman—any clergyman—performing the ceremony in his own home.

Every clergyman's family knows of such weddings. The unexpected ring at the front door during the evening. The maid coming up to announce that there's a couple wanting to get married downstairs. If they've brought no witnesses (and they seldom do) members of the clergyman's family must pinch hit. A little thrill of interest runs through the house as things are gotten ready.

Usually the bridegroom pays a fee of two or three, or as much as five dollars. The clergyman, according to custom, gives it to his wife.

I had often been a witness at such a wedding and I thought this would be the best way for me to be married, but in whose house? Because, of course, Papa would be unwilling to perform it. I would be unwilling too, for it seemed to me that my father positively hated Kent.

I knew most of the Brooklyn clergy. They were always at each other's houses, talking and laughing in their loud jolly voices. I had sat on their knees and laughed at their stories and jokes. But obviously it couldn't be one of Papa's Brooklyn friends.

Then I thought of the Parks family, who had spent a

summer at Digby when we were there. Dr. Parks was the rector of Calvary Church in Gramercy Square, New York. I had remained good friends with them, and when I first became engaged to Kent and began to take him around and introduce him to my friends, the Parkses were one of the first I took him to see. They had liked him at once, even the overpowering Mrs. Parks. I thought how wonderful it would be if Dr. Parks would marry us in his house.

Sunapee was as gay as usual that summer. There were water sports, picnics on the islands; the lake was dotted with sailboats, rowboats, canoes. In the evenings there was the sound of music drifting over the water, voices mingling with the sound of banjo or guitar.

Kent came up for weekends and proved as skillful at paddling a canoe as he was at driving a motorcar. Once when there was a storm on the lake and high choppy waves, he brought a canoe in from one of the islands, standing up in the middle of it, his feet braced apart, his arms swinging the paddle in long sweeps from front to back. The canoe simply danced from one wave to the next. People watched from the shore, expecting to see the little skiff overturn any minute. No one else could do such a thing.

Matrigna invited Kent to the house when Papa was not there and when other young people were coming. He would sit on the porch, sipping iced tea and yelling disconcerting remarks at the players on the tennis court.

I saw that summer all the girls were crazy about him. That did not surprise me, but there were older women who were attracted to him as well. Years later even my staid and dignified cousin was to say to me, "He is the thrillingest man I have ever met."

I had made the complete, headlong plunge into ecstasy! When we had first met he had not so thrilled me. Of course I had been impressed by his extraordinary good looks but I remembered how I had avoided him and palmed him off on Bess. I remembered the "No" I tried to say to him so many times. It was not so much that I was thrilled by him—it was that he had simply taken possession of me. Mastered me.

In the evenings he often took me out on the lake in a canoe. He filled the bottom of it with cushions and I curled up on them in the center while he sat in the stern, paddling with just that bend and twist of his body that made it shoot so easily through the water.

One evening he nosed the canoe into the shallows and we rocked there comfortably, half hidden among the reeds, watching a big lopsided moon rise. As the evening wore on I lay in his arms as he held me to him. Occasionally there was the splash of a fish leaping out of the water; the sudden chorus of frogs croaking. The moon began to glow.

I lifted one of Kent's hands and looked at it. I had always thought his hands at variance with his big masculine body. They were long, slender and beautiful hands, more like a woman's.

He said, "I'd make you my wife now but for the terrible risk to you."

He said it quite coolly, seeming not at all carried away, and it was lucky for he was not. Nothing like this had ever happened to me before and I was under a spell.

The summer at Lake Sunapee ended but not the cold war between Papa and me. Soon after we returned to Brooklyn I went over to see Dr. Parks and made my request.

We had quite a long talk. Of course he knew Papa and was puzzled by his attitude. I answered his questions as honestly as I could. At last he agreed to marry us.

As soon as I got home I told Papa and it simply bowled him over. He couldn't get over it. He kept repeating "Parks? Parks?"

I ended by telling him that he needn't be afraid there would be anything shady about my marriage. No elopement with a license at the city hall. But when I got to my own room, I put my head in my pillow and cried from sheer misery and exhaustion. I had a queer feeling that he would have liked the elopement better than Dr. Parks.

Sometime after the talk with him about Dr. Parks, Papa came to my room one afternoon and said, "Let's bury the hatchet."

I was overjoyed. A miserable weight was lifted from my heart. I threw myself into his arms. But when I drew back and looked happily into his face I saw the strangest expression there, something devious. My joy subsided. I became doubtful.

"This isn't because—you don't mean I shouldn't have Dr. Parks marry us?"

He had the look of a person saying one thing and meaning another.

"Oh, of course, whichever you wish, but it would look better if I did it."

So he got his way.

I wore my going-away suit of brown velveteen; Kent, a frock coat I had never seen before, buttoned very tight around his slim height. Matrigna added a touch of festivity to the occasion by putting a vase of big yellow chrysanthemums on the piano against which we were to stand.

My darling brother, Reese, held my hand tight all through the ceremony and answered, "I do" when Papa asked, "Who giveth this woman to be married to this man?"

Everything was smooth and solemn and correct.

After the ceremony an unforgettable thing happened. But it is embarrassing, particularly as Matrigna had presented me with a wedding present that must have cost several hundred dollars: a solid silver salad bowl, beautifully chased around the top. Papa came to me and said, "Mister Parrot has given me a very handsome wedding fee—twenty dollars. I will give you that for your wedding present. Would you like me to buy something for you with it or would you rather have the money?"

I said I would rather have the money, and he handed me the crisp new twenty-dollar bill which had so recently been in Kent's pocket.

Incredible.

Very joyously Kent and I sped out of the house, headed eventually for the north woods. Our first stop was the Waldorf Hotel in Manhattan. Later we stopped at Elma's Westport cottage, where she had thought we might spend a week or so. Here I discovered how thoroughly my Papa had washed his hands of me, for there was a letter.

My mother had left a trust fund of ten thousand dollars for the four of us, which Papa was to control and disburse for our education as he saw fit. He now saw fit to make my share over to me. The check was in the envelope.

Our honeymoon was going to be just what Kent had promised. The fact that the woods would be snow-covered and the rivers frozen just made it more exciting. How much Kent would have to teach me! I did not even know how to snow-shoe.

How gentle he was. I remember a night when we stopped at a backwoods hotel and the only bed was so narrow Kent had to hold me to keep me from falling out. He held me all night. It seemed to me that he did not sleep at all himself but spent the night watching over me.

My young husband gave me no tiaras or diamond necklaces but he did find for me a hood made of mink which reached down to my eyebrows in front, loose enough at the neck for a turtleneck sweater to be pulled up to my nose. Four lines of frost-fringed eyelashes ornamented the rest of my face and a coat collar rising above my ears framed it all.

We went over the border into Canada toward Lake St. John and found a man, a M. Henri Dubois, who seemed to have been located there just for our needs and convenience. He had a cosy little hotel. He owned everything in sight, and he had strings of camps for American tourists who came up to fish or hunt and all the equipment that they would need. We decided to spend the winter there.

Reese was studying law at Columbia University that winter, but he could not resist the call of the wild when we wrote him to come up for the Christmas holidays.

Kent and Reese thought it would be fun to get a moose. M. Dubois made all the arrangements: the exact place we must go to, what we must carry with us. I remember one night thirty below zero, when I slept between the two in a small tent. Kent was next to the stove, which he had to stoke at intervals all night long.

They never did shoot a moose but that morning we found the tracks of one quite close to the tent. He had ringed it completely, stopping at one place, apparently, to sniff at the queer thing.

When Reese left, M. Dubois gave us a cosy little cabin all to ourselves with a French-Canadian maid to do our chores. In the evenings Kent and I would play chess. I never won a game from him. And whenever he made the last move that cornered me and burst into his loud uproarious laugh, I would become furious. I do not see how anyone who puts his heart into a game can be a good loser. I was not. I would stalk away from him in icy dignity.

One thing I learned during those games of chess was that Kent was thinking not about a career with cars and engines, which he did so easily and so well, but about the profession of law and eventually politics. I was amazed. He was three years older than Reese and had not yet taken the first step toward such a career. Did he have any natural bent for it as he had the feel for an engine? Then I remembered how invincible he was at chess, a game which demands brains and a mastery of strategy. Strategy is needed in politics too.

Kent refused to waste time going to law school—he would just take some special courses and then the bar exams. I wondered what was going to bring all this about, but I had confidence in Kent. He did not seem to be a man who would fail to get what he wanted.

The one disappointment of my honeymoon was the physical relationship. Being romantic, I had expected to find it enjoyable, but I did not and was astonished at Kent's enthusiasm. It seemed to me it had been greatly over-idealized by poets and novelists and this, probably, because it was nature's way of producing the next generation.

Well—I wanted children. I resolved that Kent should never know how I felt. After all, it seemed at the time much worse for him than me. Humiliating—almost insulting. Nor would I let it prey on my mind. What matter one small misery beside so many joys.

Often I lay awake for hours, listening to the sounds in the forest, mysterious and incomprehensible. A sharp crack, like a rifle shot, a long silence, a swishing sound, a tap, tap, tap. Once a scream like the terrible shriek of a woman being murdered made me sit bolt upright. It hardly woke Kent. He drew me down again. "Just a panther," he said.

Then the spring came and the ice broke up with cracks and booms such as I had never heard before except when it was thundering. The rivers and streams began to flow. Loons spread their immense white wings and flapped down the lake, screaming.

Fishermen appeared at the hotel and were busy with M. Dubois inspecting bamboo poles, gut leaders, reels and flies. A good many guides were on hand, thin sunburned men who spoke a sort of patois, half French, half English.

Kent was in his element, picking just the right lightweight rod for me, the cork handle, and he never got tired of studying the flies, picking out the right ones to entice the trout. He was going to teach me to fly-fish and show me a pool where you could cast in your line and the water would "boil" with leaping rainbow trout.

I was an apt pupil. Soon I could cast almost as well as he. We went on quite long trips with a couple of guides to make the portages and carry the stuff we needed.

That first year of our marriage was all playtime, but not the second.

We returned to Cambridge, where Kent felt he could prepare himself for the law. Do the necessary study in the library of our small apartment. Attend court sessions. Cultivate the right people. He had an old friend there, Judge Byron, with whom he would play pinochle on Sunday afternoons.

This was the stronghold of the Parrots. I never knew such people for telling everybody else what to do, although Kent was a bit like that himself. There were a number of older brothers and sisters, a raft of in-laws and many young nieces and nephews.

Early in 1908, the following year, I discovered I was pregnant, and we returned to New York and took rooms in the Gramercy Park Apartment Hotel.

By mid-September the weather was scorchingly hot and I was as big as a house. I couldn't take the long cool tub baths I wanted because if I got into the tub I couldn't get out. So Kent steadied me with one hand, and with the other sponged me down, pouring dippersful of water around my neck to run deliciously down my body. Kent was very patient with me.

11

The Little Star

The New York Lying-in Hospital was quite near Gramercy Park, a great convenience to us, as our friends, the Parks, had taken Kent in while I was at the hospital. I was already installed in a large sunny room in the private pavilion on the fifth floor under the care of Dr. Davis, for I had been having what he called false pains for two weeks.

I was sick and tired of waiting. I felt like an invaded and occupied country and I longed for the "delivery"—a very good word for it, I thought.

Kent visited me every evening and spent his days working at his old headquarters, the uptown West Side Garage. It was brilliant October weather and he would walk from the Parkses' without overcoat or hat.

For men to dress for dinner was not universally done even in the best social circles in America, but the Parkses did and Kent was often in his well-tailored tuxedo.

Having a baby, I had always thought, was sort of an athletic stunt. In spite of being the delicate one of the family, I was good at athletics. I could play tennis, swim a

mile, climb mountains. I was the right age, limber and
strong, as well as double jointed. That might help too. Just
unjoint, then hook up again. I expected no trouble.

Elma visited often. Her year delivering babies in the
slum tenements provided her with very funny stories
indeed. Especially the way the women shrieked, "Oi-yoi!
Oi-yoi!" Depending on how loud the shrieking was Elma
knew if she could walk up the many flights of stairs or
would have to run.

There would be no "Oi-yois" from me. As for the
pain, everyone had had some of it at the hands of dentists
and doctors and it was certainly awful. But I prided myself
on being as stoical as an Indian and would seldom let even
an "Ouch" escape me.

One morning Dr. Davis made me stay in bed. He
took measurements, listened with his stethoscope on one
side of my body, then the other.

"Let her rest all she can today. She's going to need her
strength tomorrow. Keep the room quiet. Draw the
curtains."

By afternoon the pains were coming regularly, about
five minutes apart, and the sleeping I did was between
them, fathoms deep sleep.

The next day was quite different

"Keep her walking. Don't let her stop."

And there was a nurse on each side of me forcing me
up and down the room. I pleaded with them, "Oh, I
can't—I can't—oh, no—"

When the doctor came in, I begged "No, no, Dr.
Davis—I can't go on—let me stop—let me rest—"

"Keep walking Mrs. Parrot, it helps—it's the best
thing for you."

"Dr. Davis. I don't want the baby, I've changed my
mind."

Silence from the doctor and more helpless moans from
me, for the exhaustion that enwrapped me was not just a
lack of strength but a leaden blanket that was dragging me

down into a bottomless pit of quicksand. I lost all track of time. Had it been one day and night? Another day?

There was a sharp rap on the door. The nurse opened it to admit a couple of orderlies wheeling in a stretcher. They put me on it and wheeled me rapidly along many corridors. Blankets covered me, even my face.

We arrived at the delivery room. Dr. Davis came to my side and took my hand. There were a number of nurses and interns in the room, all doing something. The room was blazing with lights.

When I began to scream they put a sheet twisted into a rope for me and told me to pull against that. They called it "bearing down." But it gave me no purchase.

Miss Bustard, the head nurse, a big rock of a woman, took her place at the head of the table, behind me. I reached my arms up and wrapped them around her, bearing down and screaming terribly. That went on a long time. No such screams had ever before emerged from the Lying-in Hospital. They were heard down at Hicks Street which was six blocks away.

I pulled Miss Bustard down until she was bent double over me. She roared with laughter and it did me good to hear her. My screams leaped up an octave. I was trying to force out of myself something that was lodged in me, clinging with the strength of a rooted oak tree.

Down at Hicks Street people stopped and turned, listening, then saw the lighted windows of the Lying-in Hospital and walked on, slowly.

I smelled chloroform but could not inhale because my breath was all going out in the screams. At last came oblivion.

A wave of excitement ran through the hospital. "Have you seen the little star in the private pavilion? You never saw such a beauty. Twelve pounds—she looks six months old—"

This was my daughter. Everyone who could make a

pilgrimage to the fifth floor to see her did so. As long as we were in the hospital she was never called anything but the "little star." She was truly beautiful. Not red and wrinkled, but a skin of cream with a faint pink flush on cheeks and lips.

She had a small crown like a halo, very fair, faintly tinged with reddish gold.

Dr. Davis stood beside me holding the bundle of blankets in his arms and showed her to me.

"A real beauty," he said simply.

But a strange shock ran through me. She had been a part of me for so long that I expected to see, somehow, a small replica of myself. She was nothing of the sort. She was a complete stranger to me. I had never known or seen anyone in the least like her.

When Kent came to pay his evening visit he went first to the nursery. The nurses put the little star in his arms, and watched and tittered as he took her, fitting her into the crook of his left elbow, the soft fuzz of her pale gold hair lying back against the satin lapel of his dinner jacket.

"Mr. Parrot come to see his baby," they whispered.

The little star nestled against him, seeming well content to be there. From the first there was an affinity between them.

Once in my room, whether or not she had recently been fed, he wanted to see me nurse her. In those days the feminine garment called a brassiere had not been invented. To control the first rush of milk, a simple bandage was used, wrapped tight around the breast and fastened with safety pins. Kent removed this, put the baby in proper position and sat down to watch us.

Once he said, "I wish I could do that."

When the time came that I could go out for a walk with Kent, he said, "Now I've got my little woods maiden back again."

Of the visitors from Brooklyn, Reese came first, while I was giving the baby her lunch. When I heard the knock on the door, I pulled the sheet over the baby's head. In Europe I had often seen women nursing their babies in public places—parks, crowded trams, even in social gatherings. But never in this country.

Whenever my brother and I met after a long absence or a significant experience it was a high moment. He leaned over and kissed me. "Where is she? The nurse told me you had the baby in here with you." I pulled the sheet back.

That scene, surely the one most often painted by religious artists, is familiar to all. What was unfamiliar was the way the baby opened her eyes wide to look at him, without interrupting her feeding, big browny-blue eyes wavering but seeking. Surely that was curiosity. We both laughed.

The second caller was Elma, who made a flying visit up from Philadelphia. They had put a bassinet in the room with me now so I could have the baby when I wanted. Elma pounced on the bassinet, dragged the baby out of it with half the blankets and proceeded to galumph around the room with her just to show how nonchalant she was about babies.

I protested, I implored, finally I burst into tears and rang for the nurse.

Papa was the last to come.

The nurse was impressed as she announced the handsome reverend gentleman and hurried to make the room tidy, smoothing the bed, plumping the pillows and propping me up against them with a fresh bed jacket on.

Papa kissed me casually, asked how I was, sat down and made conversation. I waited for some sign of affection or of his being ready to be my father again, but there was none. I was very embarrassed, and I supposed he might be too. He said nothing about the baby's baptism, did not even ask me what we would name her. Perhaps all that would come after he had seen her, I thought, so I rang for the nurse to take him to the nursery and show the baby to him. But while he was gone, a cloud of doubts swarmed over me.

Suppose he didn't desire a reconciliation? That chill I had felt while he was sitting beside me—a real blight—suppose that had come to stay? Suppose he had never even begun to accept Kent as his son-in-law? How then could the baby be his grandchild, how could I ever again be even his prodigal daughter?

My fears gave rise to far-reaching changes—extensive travels. I thought of the University of California at Los Angeles and a home near there for us instead of here in New York. A cloud of ill-will gave me an actual pain in my heart.

When Papa came back and said, as he would to any other member of his congregation when he didn't know what to say, "Well that *is* a baby!" I realized the die was cast.

Before Christmas of 1908 we were settled in Los Angeles.

The little star had been baptized before we left New York, but not in St. Ann's. That was performed in Calvary Church on Gramercy Park and by Dr. Parks, who lifted her up as high as he could to let the congregation see her, as was his habit. Before we left, Mrs. Parks gave me a letter of introduction to an old schoolmate of hers who now lived in Los Angeles.

"She will know everyone worth knowing," she said as she handed it to me. I put it away carefully.

Kent and my father, after passing the twenty-dollar bill from one to the other at the wedding, never saw each other again.

PART TWO

12

Porter, Morgan, and Parrot

It is a fairly common experience in life to want something ardently, set your heart on it, get it, then find you are not happy with it after all. Something is missing. Or your aim was wrong. Or something unpleasant is attached to it.

In California, that first year, I had got what I had struggled so hard to win, and yet was miserably unhappy.

It was not merely dissatisfaction. How could it be that? I loved my tall and handsome husband and was proud of him. He was as arresting, as masterful, as eye-catching as ever. O'Hara was the most bewitching baby; caring for her and her tiny garments was a delight. I had bought a big white wicker perambulator for her and spent much of my time wheeling her about in it. Southern California was the garden spot it was reputed to be, the air perfumed with the scent of roses and geraniums.

There were many little parks with comfortable benches under shade trees. I would find an empty one, set the brake on the pram, sit down and take out my sewing and conduct a searching probe into the causes of my misery.

Of course I missed the big noisy Brooklyn house, people coming and going, the front door bell ringing, the clatter and chatter, someone practicing the piano. But that was just a bit of homesickness such as a girl would feel when she went away to boarding school. No. Something must be wrong with our whole situation here, and yet we had been very careful planning it.

We had chosen a good family hotel on a quiet, tree-shaded street. It was in a good neighborhood and only a few blocks from a tram line that led straight to the university. On that conveyance Kent left every morning for the university and returned in time for dinner.

The dean of the law school, Nicholas Porter, also taught a few classes. Kent was in his class in torts and they got to be friends. Mr. Porter was a bachelor and had lived all his life in Los Angeles. He knew everybody and belonged to all the clubs. I remembered what Kent had said about always getting to know the right people, and wondered how he did it. He certainly cultivated the friendship with Mr. Porter.

Mr. Porter already had one young law student, Ted Morgan, at a desk in his office, running legal errands for him. In the back of our minds we hoped perhaps he would take another, Kent Parrot, and eventually there would be three names on the door of a well-known law firm.

There was nothing I would want to change. Everything was just the way we had planned it, or even better, but my unhappiness was so deep and so despairing it felt as if it would last forever, as if I had taken some terribly fatal step.

It was true that I had gone against my father, but thousands of girls have done that. No guilt there. Well, was there guilt anywhere? And, of course, then I began to think about that incompatability in our physical relationship, which had never changed. But I could not blame myself for that. Nor Kent either. No one except nature herself, who had arranged things this way. The man had to be the aggressor, the woman had to yield. It was even legal. Her recompense would be in the children she would have. This was the prudish mid-Victorian theory, a theory I had never agreed with, thanks to my brother Reese's coaching. When Reese had showed me a passage in an unexpurgated edition of the *Arabian Nights* which stated that woman's urge was fiercer than man's, I felt that marriage was going to be very exciting. Now here I was, feeling that the Victorians were right.

Yet I knew there were women who derived pleasure from sex. This puzzled me. And what a misfortune for a man to take his bride home and find she didn't want him in that way. Just those circumstances which aroused desire in him aroused in me only the desire to escape if I decently could, though of course I decently could not. Not because I was legally his and had to, but because I loved him and pitied him and wanted to be kind and fair to him.

I hid my unwillingness, and, to smother the least outcry of protest, sank my teeth into my forearms. Even so, as he would walk away from me the room would be filled with the violence of his cursing, and at breakfast we could hardly speak to each other.

This did cast a sort of shadow over my life, especially when I looked at the tooth marks on my arms and could not wear short-sleeved blouses. But it was not enough to cause my unhappiness. I was philosophical. One had to put up with some things. Suppose I had rheumatism—something that hurt all the time.

I gave up searching for reasons, the analyses, philosophizings, and let my thoughts drift to the surface, wander, just day-dreaming.

But it was not day-dreaming, for there was no invention in it. It was pure reminiscing, a reliving of past experiences. Again the Brooklyn house. I took pleasure in remembering even those long dull Sundays when nearly everything was a boring duty, except perhaps the hymns in church. Clothes were different on Sundays: different when one bought them, hung them away for Sunday wear only, then the wearing of them and comparing them in church with everyone else's. Hats were in a special category and could entertain one through an entire sermon.

I realized there were other things in my life I was missing. Kent and I had not joined a church here or even given such a thing a thought.

I missed the athletics, too, the sports and games I was so fond of and so good at. And the dancing—oh! the dancing!

I was born with a keen susceptibility to movement. Just why the matching of rhythmic movements of the body to rhythmic beats of music should produce such intoxicating pleasure was a mystery. My addiction to it had begun when I was four.

Thinking of dancing, I thought of Mr. Dodsworth, our dancing master.

Our weekly lesson was on Saturday afternoons.

Mr. Dodsworth was always formally dressed in cutaway and striped trousers. He wore gloves and held a clapper which he smacked into the palm of his left hand to give the signals to the band and the dancers.

Boys did not like dancing as well as girls (when they were small) and often got out of going, so quite often there were more girls than boys. When this happened girls could dance with girls. Elma and I always rushed for each other. Though she was four years older than I, we were nearly the same height. She was good at leading, I at following. We loved to dance together because we were the best dancers on the floor.

On one occasion Mr. Dodsworth stopped the music and ordered us all back to our seats. Then he ordered Elma and me to take our places in the middle of the floor again and signaled the music to begin. A solo dance! The full

band was playing just for Elma and me! In the Pierrepont
Assembly Rooms!

The dance was called the schottische, which Mr.
Dodsworth had just finished teaching us. We had learned it
easily, and performed it without the slightest error, gliding
forward and kicking, whirling a few times. We were
dressed in red plaid kilts, our long brown hair, as usual, in
ringlets to our waist.

When the dance ended and the music stopped, Mr.
Dodsworth put his clapper under his arm and led a round of
applause in which even the bandsmen joined.

Suddenly forcing myself back to the present, I drew a
long deep breath. How far back into the past this
reminiscing had drawn me without making me any the
wiser, unless the wisdom of seeing clearly that the life of a
social butterfly and a dancer is not the best apprenticeship
for being a young mother, washing diapers, wheeling
prams, living in strange places.

But this, I could see, was not my special misery, but
the fate of nearly every girl—to be a young mother and
nothing but that.

After such ruminations it would be nearly lunchtime
and the baby would be awake. I would lean over her to lift
her and rearrange her cushions, take the brake off and head
for home.

Home? There was no feeling of home about the hotel
for me. I hated it. Especially eating in that dining room
with twenty or thirty other people. Each family had its own
individual table. It was a big sunny room and the food was
good, but the people so different.

New Englanders, being the closest of all Americans to
old Englanders, have never got over being snobbish about
it. I wondered myself at the way these westerners looked.
Nothing like our friends in Brooklyn Heights.

And once again I began to count and calculate. Could
our income (which was still only my allowance from the

Denny Estate, for Kent was not yet earning) be stretched
enough to pay rent for a house—a little house; it need not
be big or in the fashionable neighborhoods, it need only
give us the dignity of privacy.

But there was no use kidding myself, we could not
afford a house. We barely made ends meet as it was. We
were miserably pinched for money.

Money! Why, of course. That was the whole trouble!
That was always the trouble. Everybody's trouble. Why
hadn't I thought of that before.

Even at home when we were children, whether or not
we got what we wanted and asked for was decided by
money. The cost of it. If something was big and expensive,
one child could not own it alone. Bicycles, tricycles, even
sleds and express wagons we held in common. Why?
Because we were not rich. Why weren't we? Clergymen are
never rich. Which made me wonder about the profession of
law.

But Kent had said that in the profession of law there
were all sorts of opportunities—never worry, we would be
rich all right, once he got his bar degree.

I muttered out loud that if we had all the money we
needed—wanted—I wouldn't be unhappy at all.

I stopped the pram and stood still, listening to those
words, following them to that inner chamber—a sort of
courtroom where statements were questioned, tried, and
tested. And I saw it was not true at all. There was
something basically wrong.

I began walking again, feeling that I was caught in a
trap and could not get out.

Inland from Los Angeles are many tall craggy hills. As
I wheeled the pram I lifted my eyes to those hills and
remembered words of Psalm 121: "I will lift up mine eyes
unto the hills, from whence cometh my help." But no help
came.

*   *   *

Kent's progress in his studies was something he never talked about, and when I wondered (out loud) what Mr. Porter thought of his chances of passing the bar exams, he was surprised and exclaimed, "Oh, any dumbbell could pass those!"

When the news came, it reached me by the telephone. Kent told me that the results were in—the list of those who had passed was on the board.

"Your name was one of them?"

"Why sure!"

I hung up the receiver and stood there, my heart thumping. Not long afterwards, Kent drove home from the university in a smart red roadster, drew up at the curb and proudly brought me out to look at it, saying that it was ours. When I asked him how such a car could possibly be ours, his mouth went down at the corner in that mocking twist.

"Bought and paid for! That's how."

My bewilderment grew. As if he read my mind, Kent explained, "Bought from a client. Paid for with a legal opinion."

Stupidly I repeated his words, staring at the car. "A legal opinion?"

Kent continued, "A legal opinion which saved him from a damage suit which would have ruined him."

My opinion of the law as a profession was greatly enhanced.

Also, I began to be much happier, or at least to keep those thoughts about being in a trap down under. One could have a lot of fun now that we had the roadster.

Sunday mornings we went house-hunting. I was determined to get out of that hotel. I was like the fisherman asking gifts from the genie he had caught in a bottle. As soon as the genie had given me one wish, I asked for another.

One Sunday we saw a bungalow on Juliet Street and

fell in love with it at sight. Such a bungalow is as indigenous to southern California as its canopies of climbing roses and bougainvillea. Across half of the house, reaching the bright blue door, was a bank of scarlet geraniums and there was a "For Rent" sign near the curb.

It was a long time before we got the bungalow. There was not a stick of furniture in it, just five, charming empty rooms over a basement kitchen. We could not sign the lease until I had written Mr. Shaw to inquire if funds from my trust could be made available. In the end they were.

13

Clarence and Kay

When people remarked on how quickly O'Hara picked up words and how well she pronounced them I had a laughing reply that became a joke in the family.

"Oh, she was born speaking perfect English."

She certainly did not get that from Kent, who still said breakfast as if it was spelled "breppfuss." I had been trained to speak properly as a little girl. In one corner of our dining room stood a two-branched, waist-high iron standard. A dictionary in two big volumes rested on it. Any one who, during a meal, mispronounced or misused a word, had to go to the dictionary, look up the word, and read it aloud with its proper pronunciation and definition.

One day, when O'Hara was two years old, she trotted out to the garden where a Japanese gardener was edging a border and gave him a unique example of her perfect English.

"My Mummy's going to have a baby."

He was interested, withdrew his spade, and stood leaning on it, looking down at her.

"When?" he finally asked.

She waved her hand and turned away, saying, "Coming later," and trotted back into the house where I was getting ready, in quite a hurry, to go downtown.

On the way in to me she had realized that her information on the subject was not complete. Reaching me, she asked, "Mummy, how *does* a lady have a baby?"

Almost ready to leave, I paused to look at her, "How does a chicken lay an egg?"

By the time she had the answer I had my purse and gloves in my hand, and Annie, the maid, had come in to take over.

"Gives a big try?" questioned O'Hara triumphantly.

"That's exactly right," I said, and bent to kiss her good-bye.

That spring Elma was in Vienna, Austria, taking a postgraduate course in obstetrics at the famous clinic there. We corresponded regularly, and Elma had promised that she would cross the Atlantic Ocean and the American continent in time for the arrival of my second baby if I would just be definite about the date.

I was and she did. But when she got to the bungalow she had eyes for no one but the little star, O'Hara, who, she declared, was simply impossibly beautiful. Her hair, the color of a burnished chestnut with red and gold shades in it, was in a halo of curls around her head. Her big brown eyes searched and questioned. Her mouth was like a ripe red cherry. Whoever saw her stopped to marvel at her. When children possess this voluptuous beauty they draw all eyes, like a flower or butterfly or jewel.

My obstetrician was Dr. M. L. Moore, assisted by his son, Clarence. My room was engaged at the hospital. All was in readiness.

The first thing that went wrong was that when my pains began Dr. Moore was on a maternity case in Long Beach, which is about fifty miles from Los Angeles.

Clarence Moore and Kent discussed this on the telephone. We were good friends of the young Moores— went out with them on weekend trips; drove to the beach for a swim and dinner.

The Long Beach baby had not yet arrived, and when it did, provided there were no complications, it would take Dr. Moore an hour and a half to drive to Los Angeles. Clarence's opinion was that he'd better get ready to take on the case himself.

When Kent told me this I was shocked. It seemed indecent and I made him relay a point-blank refusal to Clarence.

"Then," said Clarence, "we'll have to get another obstetrician. Dr. Peters. Or Dr. Greene. I'll telephone them right away. Or maybe Menzies. Next to Father they're the three best men in town."

Kent, already in an advanced state of the jitters, left it to Clarence.

The next hour was spent in fruitless telephone calls, for it was late Friday afternoon and, apparently, not a single doctor was at home.

Elma was timing my pains. At last she ordered Kent to bring up the car and Annie to pack my bag for the hospital. When we got there I went to my room and bed immediately while Kent took Elma to talk with Clarence, who was already in his long white linen surgeon's coat.

"I've got the delivery room ready, Dr. Alsop," he said to Elma. "How long do you think it will be?"

"Not very long. She had awfully strong pains with her first baby."

"I've not been able to find another doctor. We're still trying. This is likely to be you or me."

"Not me," said Elma. "I won't take the responsibility. I'll help you."

"All right. Go in to her now and tell me how much she's dilated."

The pains were bad now and coming faster. By the

time Clarence came to my room and told me firmly he was taking charge, I didn't care who it was. They wheeled me into the delivery room. Here were all the remembered sights: the table in the center of the room with the bank of lights blazing overhead, nurses and interns in readiness.

They had me on the table in a moment.

Clarence warned me. "Now don't bear down. It's coming too fast. You'll be torn."

I grabbed the arm of a nurse standing beside me and gritted my teeth, writhing. The head was right there. A strong, determined baby was striving to enter the world.

"Don't bear down! Hold back!" ordered Clarence again. He placed the palm of his hand against the round skull and, with all his might, held it from advancing.

Clarence was a big fellow but his whole body shook with the effort. He fought. Nature fought. Then, young elastic flesh yielded a little and the head slipped out without a tear.

What happened next startled every one. The baby's head began to yell. Nothing else emerged.

Elma talked about it later.

"They do look so funny when that happens—the head out and yelling, nothing else born yet. You know they aren't supposed to be able to do that. It takes breath to yell. Usually the whole baby is out and has to be slapped and worked over before he can yell because he can't breathe until the umbilical cord is closed off. But sometimes they find a way to do it."

The yelling continued. It was lusty and indignant. Something was impeding the process.

The baby's shoulders strained against the threshold. Clarence put his weight and might against them as he had done with the head.

"Don't bear down! Breathe in!" he commanded.

I tried but failed. Flesh tore. Clarence gave a dismayed grunt. A nurse said, "A boy."

There was no anaesthetist in the hospital that night. When Clarence sewed me up I felt every thrust of the long curved needle, the thread being pulled through flesh. I pressed my lips together; squealed; moaned.

When it was over Clarence lifted me off the table and carried me down the long corridor to my room. A nurse held the door open; he laid me gently on the bed. Then he went to the bathroom and threw up. Kent was there doing the same thing.

The outstanding performance had been the baby's yelling. He never stopped while the nurses oiled, bathed, and dressed him. Or when, still in the delivery room, they put him to bed to recover from his strenuous voyage.

Dr. Moore arrived at last, worn out with the rough, fast, fifty-mile drive from Long Beach. Elma and Clarence were sitting on the hall stairs gossiping about the obstetrical techniques of Vienna. Dr. Moore said, "That's not the new baby crying, is it? Sounds like a six-month-old child."

During my pregnancy, Dr. Moore had practically starved me in his efforts to make sure that I would not have another twelve-pound baby. I did not. He weighed eleven pounds—all skin and bone. He inherited his father's length, his extra-long big toe and his broad shoulders. I have sometimes wondered if he ever caught up on the food he ought to have had to fill out that big frame.

He stopped yelling at feeding times. As most infants do he fell asleep with the last swallow and the nurse could carry him to his bassinet.

It was at such a moment—a peaceful, quiet moment—that Kent came with O'Hara. After greeting me they went to look at the baby. The bassinet was on the other side of the room.

O'Hara said, "Please lift me up so I can see my baby brother."

Kent lifted her and they stood looking down at the sleeping baby, O'Hara's face very solemn, Kent's with a smile which grew into that familiar, mocking twist of the underlip.

The baby was certainly not beautiful. If he had any hair it was so fair as to be invisible. We had named him after his father and called him Kay for short.

"I choose O'Hara," said Kent.

At which a wave of protective love for my last-born surged through me. So be it. He would be mine.

This was the little boy acknowledged by all who ever knew him to be the most adorable child that ever was.

14

Dance to the Piper

When I am writing a book, dividing my material into chapters, I give each chapter, as you will have noticed, a title. It must express the dominant idea under which all the subsidiary ideas cluster, so that when I wish to review what I have covered, I need only glance at the titles to remember which chapter is which.

But this section I am approaching now baffles me. It comprises a few years in which so much happened, I changed course so often, fell under so many new influences that it seems impossible to include every aspect of it under one title.

I tried "The Country Club," because Mr. Porter had put us up for membership at the Los Angeles Country Club and now it became the setting for all our recreations—tennis and golf, Saturday night dinners and dances. And "The Fast Set," because this was a very fast set indeed, doing things and talking about things far beyond anything I had even known before. But all quite familiar to Kent. "The Frasers" seemed another possibility, but this would not do either for there was far too much else to tell. But as they entered our lives at that time, I shall drop the search for a title for the moment and go on with Fanny and Owen Fraser, for they became our most intimate friends, playing tennis and golf together, dining at each other's houses, going to the theater and all social functions together, taking long drives and weekend trips in their four-passenger car.

They were strangers in Los Angeles, even as we were. They had come from Chicago, not a background to recommend them to society, but Fanny was a born climber and Owen was well-heeled. They were an attractive couple.

Fanny Fraser had a letter of introduction to Mrs. Sherman, the arbitor of breeding in our social set, which happened to reach that lady the same day mine did. Mrs. Sherman called on us both, looked us over, decided in our favor and launched us at a big tea.

At that first tea I felt an arm thrust through mine, and heard a pleading voice, "Oh, do let me hang on to you. I don't know a soul in this crowd!"

"Neither do I," I muttered.

We clung together, saving each other from the horror of being solitary in the midst of a convivial crowd.

Besides, we liked each other instantly.

She was not exactly pretty, but she had a charming, piquant face with an up-turned freckled nose, ash-blond hair, and a figure hard to hold within bounds.

But it was her wit and humor and the fact that we had so much in common that drew us so quickly together. This ripened into a sisterly and confidential friendship that lasted until her death many years later.

We were amazingly compatible, both interested in the same things. Mostly watching our new friends and acquaintances, then gossiping with each other about them. Who was crazy about whom? There were many bachelors hanging around the young married women. Which was a real affair and which just a flirtation?

We had arguments. I could not believe that either a man or woman would be untrue to their marriage vows. Outrageous, flirty behavior was even a proof that everything was aboveboard between them.

"Don't you believe it!" Fanny said. "Right in this crowd we're watching there'll be some divorces."

We were both interested in literature, working at short stories, and hoped and intended to be selling to the women's magazines soon. *Cosmopolitan*, for example, printed hardly anything but love affairs—the beginnings, waxing and finally a divorce, or suddenly changing partners. They were exciting stories and such stories were going on all around us. It was a game that was being played.

So Fanny and I watched and filled our notebooks with bits of business or dialogue, even wrote samples or parts of such stories. I felt that if I could just find a good title, I'd be ready to write one now. Titles always inspire me.

Fanny had the idea that a woman must be constantly on the alert to hold her husband, which seemed to me simply laughable. As if there were sirens on all sides ready to snatch him.

"There was a story in last month's *Cosmopolitan* describing just such an affair," insisted Fanny.

Our long confabs took place in her garden or mine with our children playing in the sandpile at the far end.

We did a good deal of flirting ourselves in society. We enjoyed it. We compared our techniques in hilarious sessions, giggling like schoolgirls. Fanny made conquests by pretending to believe in fairies; I, by a silent meeting of eyes held a little too long. Or perhaps an accidental touch. To which, I admitted to Fanny, I was susceptible myself.

And I recounted to her an anecdote of my childhood. I was four. Seated on the sofa within the encircling arm of a gentleman visitor, I exclaimed, "That's right! Hug me tight!"

"Don't try it now," warned Fanny. "Cuddling is dangerous."

"But so nice."

"It's an invitation."

I disagreed. It should be taken for just what it is— human warmth and affection.

There were also other, less frivolous subjects which engrossed us, such as religion. Fanny had been brought up a Christian Scientist. I had read and been convinced by Sir Arthur Eddington that there was no such thing as matter— only a certain rate of vibration. So Fanny and I were on the same track under the general term of Subjective Idealism.

Our reading and thinking on such subjects kept pace with our dissipations. In my father's house in Brooklyn occasionally we had champagne for dinner if there was a reason for a celebration. I liked that or a glass of sherry sometimes. But until Kent taught me I had never tasted hard liquor except the whiskey in my milk when I was laid up with one of my bad colds. Now I drank something else on occasion."

At the first one Kent had said, "Don't turn your head away and make a face as if it was medicine. Drink it as if you liked it."

But it still was not the taste I liked, but the stimulation that came five minutes later. Kent instructed me further.

"Always count your drinks. Know how much you can hold without feeling it too much."

I soon knew all about that.

He taught me to gamble in the same careful way. He was a crack bridge player. I did not know it at all. The only card games I had played were a little family euchre, and before that "Old Maid" when we were children.

Kent taught me bridge by the simple method of taking me into a game with himself and two cronies. I had beginner's luck and held all the high cards but managed in spite of that to lose all the tricks. They laughed so hard when at the end of each hand I had to throw away my aces and face cards that they could hardly sit up. They howled. I howled too but I was weeping behind a little fan of cards with which I covered my face. But I learned. At the end of a year I was keeping a bridge purse and playing for a tenth of a cent a point.

When it came to dancing it was I who had to teach Kent. He had never been to dancing school, had never picked it up and had no rhythm or music in him. When he absolutely had to take someone out on the floor he walked slowly forward, shoving his partner backward and growling, perhaps under the delusion that he was humming along with the music.

At the club, whenever a new dance step came in they would get a teacher and have a class and we'd learn it. The black bottom, the turkey trot, the rumba.

Kent considered the turkey trot indecent and forbade me to dance it. I had always obeyed Kent. It was the natural thing to do. In fact, most people obeyed him because he was that kind of man. But I was years older now. Was I going to be bossed around like that for the rest of my life as if I were a child? Of course "obey" was in the marriage ceremony, too, but that wasn't meant to be taken literally.

One night I danced the turkey trot with Homer Brent.

When it was time to go home Kent was nowhere to be found. Our car was gone too and the Frasers had to take me home.

Now I have thought of that title I was looking for awhile back, one comprehensive title that would embrace all the hectic behaviors of that period of my life: "Dance to the Piper." For surely there was a piper playing and we were all jigging to his tune. It told us to do what we wanted, to seek pleasure, to have fun, the wilder the better.

And disregard conventions, sage advice, even danger signals. As the years went by, one, two, three, the tune was the same but the pace quickened.

It soon became quite a common occurrence for Kent to stay away from home for dinner. Just at the hour, the cook downstairs ready to dish up and the maid to serve, the telephone would ring, his excuse being just "business," or, quite as often, a card game he couldn't possibly leave.

I would just call up one of my beaux. The bachelors were always hoping for invitations to dine at private homes. A pleasant dinner, then the visit to the nursery to see the children, in their white night drawers, kneeling down to say their prayers. My visitor would leave before ten and I would spend the rest of the long evening on the couch, reading.

Fanny said with her dry humor, "All very touching. Especially the prayers in night drawers, letting him feel as if he was the daddy."

I protested, laughing, "Oh, just giving him a touch of family life. Do him good."

"And what time does your husband get home?"

"Oh, one o'clock. Sometimes two or three. And usually in a vile humor. I'm afraid he's drinking too much."

I did not tell her that when he came in late like that his favorite greeting to me as I lay on the couch was to seize my skirts at the bottom and zip them up over my head.

"My dear, if my husband left me alone as much as yours does, there would be only one queston I'd ask—who is she?"

"Stop making all those nasty insinuations about my husband."

"He's on the loose. Everyone in town knows it but you."

"Well then, *you* tell *me*. Who is she?"

Fanny heaved a sigh of relief. "Going to face facts at last! It's not *she*, da-a-arlin' (she had a way of curling her lips around the word that was very funny), it's *them*. Those floozies down at the end of the loop. Lots of them. I wouldn't know their names."

This made me laugh. I didn't take her seriously. Anyway, in that crowd, being talked about didn't mean a thing. I was talked about myself.

Someone said of me, "I hope that girl is happy because if she's not, she'll paint the town red." I was not happy and, in my own way, I proceeded to paint the town red.

For instance, the Watling affair.

Colonel Watling was much older than I but he had the finish and aplomb characteristic of the military man which seems to make them ageless and, so often, more attractive than other men. He was also a superb dancer and on the lookout for a partner equal to himself.

Mrs. Watling, who looked older than he, though you never can tell, seldom danced. She preferred bridge, and usually found a game in the card room.

I had found, in dancing, that if I turned my head sideways and imperceptibly moved it a half inch closer to my partner, my cheek would touch the cloth that covered his shoulder, and then there would be a slight tightening of his arms as if he gathered me closer. At that my response was not to move but simply to relax. And then, if he was a good dancer and kept time, our two bodies would move as one, in unison, and it was the sweetest thing in the world. I could have danced forever.

The first time Colonel Watling asked me to dance I assented indifferently. He was too old to interest me and not really handsome at all. But what a dancer! It was an experience for me, one of those blissful experiences. I was hungry for more.

As for him, after two or three Saturday nights, I realized he was dancing with no one but me. He would disappear, or wait on the sidelines until I was free again.

Fanny told me people were watching us, suspecting it was a real affair.

"They couldn't be so silly," I replied.

"It's the way you go into his arms when he asks you to dance."

"But everybody does that."

One afternoon, quite late, Colonel Watling came to call on me.

This bored me. To have to sit and make conversation with a middle-aged man when I would much rather be playing the piano.

He came again and again.

Kent came in, once, when the colonel was there. He made drinks and we had a nice little party. The colonel often brought me presents. Books, flowers, a box of chocolates.

Fanny was right. People were beginning to talk about us. The thing that made them think it was a real affair was Mrs. Watling's jealousy. She talked about me, resenting the fact that her rival for her husband's affection was so young. It is true, she was very faded with no hint of youthfulness left.

Then she did a terrible thing. She had her face lifted.

In those days there were no trained plastic surgeons to alter faces by cutting and reshaping and stitching. It was done by injections of paraffin under the skin which filled all the wrinkles and hollows and so presented a smooth, youthful appearance.

Unfortunately the paraffin sometimes shifted in very hot weather and could so alter the contours that the face would be disfigured.

This happened to Mrs. Watling. Her face became lopsided and could never be corrected. Thereafter she was never seen without a hat and a heavy blue chiffon veil.

I think it is a sad story, quite tragic.

Through Mrs. Watling's friends, who would have done better not to talk about it, it was reported that nothing Mrs. Watling did or did not do would have made any difference because her husband was really and seriously in love with Molly Parrot. They held I was the villain in the affair because I had made him fall in love, or, at least, let him. I was a flirt, a heartless little b___ and it was all my fault.

Fanny and I argued about it. Fanny insisted that, but for me, Mrs. Watling would still have had her original face.

I had, I conceded, been indiscreet. That was all, but I remembered the biblical verse, "A fair woman without discretion is like a jewel in a swine's snout." I quoted it to Fanny and we both laughed. Perhaps I had learned a little from this episode.

After a year, the Watlings moved away.

Then there was the affair I had with a flying machine and a man named Orville Wright.

It was Sunday and everyone was at the club when Orville Wright's flying machine came rolling up the eighteenth fairway and stopped.

Soon there was a crowd around it for recently newspapers had been bursting with news about what the Wright brothers had been doing. Mr. Wright was besieged with questions.

When he asked, "Would anyone like a whirl?" of course it was I who stepped forward.

Although I was considered a daredevil, I was not without fear. I feared riptides, bad undertows, bulls, high places, and quicksands. Still, danger had always had an attraction for me. It challenged one to escape and added a spice of excitement to a real-life adventure just as it did in a story.

Provided there was no objection from my husband,

Mr. Wright would be delighted to take me up. I knew Kent was out on the links so I just pretended to search for him and came back with Charley Brimmer, who unhesitatingly gave the necessary permission.

Today I cannot think of that little mousetrap as even a cousin of the winged ships that circle the globe. It looked like something teenaged boys would concoct in their own backyard out of a lot of wire and canvas and a few bicycles.

You saw at once the inventor's aim had been to keep it as light, as small, as fragile as possible so that there would be less weight to be airborne. There was, of course, no cab or roof, just the two little seats, one behind the other, in front of the first one a small dashboard with a few dials on it. Two spread wings that looked as if they were made of canvas—perhaps they were, stretched out on each side. I don't know where the engine was.

Suddenly it started with a deafening roar. We were moving. Accelerating in a cyclone of noise. Then we were flying, but the clamor did not lessen.

Mr. Wright wished to converse and point out matters of interest. The only way he could do that was to punch me in the back to get my attention, put his mouth close to my ear, and yell loud as he could. In this way he asked me if I was all right—not scared? I said I was all right and not scared; a most unfortunate lie for he zoomed up sharply, then yelled into my ear, "One thousand feet."

I don't remember any belt or straps holding me in. My feet were hanging over empty space. Finally he circled down and landed nearly right where we had started.

This exploit got me talked about. A shameless trick, they said, prevaricating to Mr. Wright to get him to take her up. But the worst was my irresponsibility as a mother. To take such a risk when I had small children to think of was reprehensible.

And now we come to the Ferguson affair.

I wanted to learn tap dancing. Usually I could pick up

new dance steps just by watching someone perform. But not tap dancing. I watched the loose fling of the foot, the way the ankle seemed unjointed; listened to the sharp clacks of the toes, right on the beat or on a syncopated fraction of the beat, tried and tried it. I could not do it, could not even figure it out.

It was quite a craze at that time. People were taking lessons to learn it. I resolved to do the same. I would only need a few.

I heard of a man at Gander Beach who had once been a professional tap dancer, but was now too old to continue. He gave lessons at $3.50 an hour. He lived in an apartment hotel and gave the lessons right in his room with a phonograph to provide the music.

All very convenient, I thought, so I telephoned him, made arrangements and drove down to the beach Thursday mornings. His name was Ferguson.

One night Kent asked, "What do you do when you go down to Gander Beach Thursdays?"

I was annoyed, knowing that I would get no sympathy from him about anything that had to do with dancing.

I said shortly, "Nothing that would be of any interest to you."

"Well then, I'll tell you," said Kent.

I laughed, "How could you?"

"Because I've had you followed by a detective and I have his report. You go to the Seaview Hotel down there and up to a man's room."

I burst out laughing. The idea of a romantic entanglement with Mr. Ferguson was so funny. I could not help it.

But a detective! Had me followed by a detective! My laughter stopped abruptly. Kent was accusing me of infidelity to him. He believed that. And this meant he would do such things himself. No doubt had *done* them.

There was an easy chair behind me. As if I had been knocked down I fell into it and stared at him. Not everyone

would be convinced by it, but to me this was incontroverti-
ble evidence. He was judging me by himself.

My thoughts traveled back in a long retroactive
survey. This would explain so much. All the things I had
heard from Fanny and the others. So many discrepancies in
his excuses and absences, and lies. Sometimes this miasma
of deceit had created such tension between us that I fled the
house. One evening when Kent was taking a telephone call
in the back hall I slipped out of the front door and ran to
the corner amazed at the sudden sense of escape and
freedom. I felt unchained!

When I returned I found Kent in a state of shock. He
gasped, "I went into the living room and you were gone!"

And I replied, "I just had to catch a breath of air." It
had happened often since.

Now I understood everything. It was as if the book of
our marriage, quite a long book, had been laid open before
me and in the single minute I had been sitting there, I had
read it from beginning to end. It was a type of marriage
which society condones—polygamy for the man, provided
appearances are kept up.

The thought of divorce crossed my mind, but I could
not repudiate Kent without repudiating O'Hara and Kay.
They were part of him and part of me.

"Well?" said Kent sharply. There was a break in his
voice, almost a croak. I had heard that before when he was
jealous. For no matter what his own infidelities, he didn't
want me to look at another man.

I knew nothing of jealousy, having never felt it, but,
apparently, it was an agonizing emotion. Kent was probably suffering terribly, and suddenly I was sorry for him.

I stood up, laughing lightly. "I'd like a breath of air
before I go to bed." I took a step or two towards the door.

Kent stared at me with an expressionless poker face
which never changed as I went on, "I hope you won't go

down to that hotel at Gander Beach and make a grease spot of that poor old Mr. Ferguson. He's taught me to tap dance so nicely. I'll show you sometime." I reached the front door, unfastened it and escaped.

15

Lions and Tigers

We recovered from that fight as we had recovered from others. To make sure that Kent believed me I had volunteered more information about Mr. Ferguson, everything I knew in fact: that he lived on the fourth floor of that hotel and gave lessons all day long. Kent could verify all this with his detective if he wanted.

But the big change was in me. My eyes had been opened. I could not unsee what I had seen or unknow what I now knew. I wondered how I could have been blind for so long. To look ahead was unnerving. When Kent lied to me I had to pretend to believe him. It was the only thing left for us to do together.

Keeping up appearances requires unremitting effort when the natural means of communication between two people has been cut off. Now there was an invisible barrier between Kent and me, dividing us.

Pretense was abhorrent to me. Now I seemed immersed in it. The evenings were the worst, unless we had guests for dinner. Then everything went well. A game of bridge could last until all hours. But when we were alone!

I could not help being, in some way, on guard against him. I once heard a woman say that when she had to go into a room where her husband was waiting, it felt as if she was entering a cage of lions and tigers.

Kent would bury himself in a popular magazine—his favorite reading. His big Morris chair was shoved into the far corner of the room, a table beside it with a bottle of scotch, the siphon of soda, his tall glass. At the other end of the room was the sofa and here I would fling myself down. The upholstered end and a cushion lifted my head so that I could read. Then silence. The long evening. We had nothing to say to each other.

Sometimes we went out in the car for a drive—there was still that one thing we could do. It was pleasant to drift about the many tree-shaded dirt roads that linked the little villages and settlements outside of Los Angeles. And Kent was as much the expert in handling a car as he had always been. I could relax, close my eyes, feel the balmy air on my face and smell the tang of the big pepper trees that spread their black shadows in the moonlight, and let my thoughts drift back to happier days when I had a husband who loved and cherished me. How could so deep a change ever have come about? So gentle he had been—so tender.

Was that the same man I was married to now? How close we had been then—how far apart now.

The barrier I had felt, the partition dividing us, was almost palpable. It was like something that could not possibly be removed. I no longer had any knowledge of his actions: where he was, what he did with his time, or whom he was with.

There were other rides too unpleasant to describe. If, as Tolstoi says, every man is seven men, one of Kent's must have been a poltergeist, for he sometimes made the ride, from first to last, an occasion for tormenting me.

In such moods he would be full of rough jokes and

that laugh of his which, at its worst—loud, raucous, and gibing—made one cringe.

My gasp of alarm at an intersection and a near collision once inspired that laugh, as well as his favorite shout of triumph, "Got your goat, didn't I?"

He made the car leap from side to side for no reason, and when I complained, roared with laughter.

"Why, that's the shimmy. The latest dance step."

I learned to clench my teeth and make no sound, whatever he did.

I wondered if this was to be my life from now on; I wondered how long I could stand it. Or perhaps it was he who wanted a divorce and was trying to make me get one.

Does a man imagine that such actions are to be accepted as the playfulness of high spirits? Does he not know that if there are sparks of love for him left in his wife's affection, he is stamping them out, one by one. That was when I began to think of divorce in quite a different way.

I thought more and more often of divorce. Men and women were not held forever in an unhappy marriage, even when there were children. I wondered if my father would countenance it under the circumstances or would just remind me that he had warned me, and now I had made my bed and must lie on it.

I thought of the biblical parable: "I will arise and go to my father." I did not do quite that, but I wrote and told him what I was considering. He replied, "Come home and tell me about it. Stay a month. Bring the children."

And so I went home. I need not have worried about my family's reactions. Their arms were held wide to receive me and no one said, "I told you so." Papa was as dead set against his son-in-law as he had ever been. I even suspect him of deriving satisfaction from the thought of taking Kent Parrot's wife and children away from him.

I returned to Los Angeles with my mind made up. I would get a divorce.

When Kent met us at the station, I could not look at him. I think that told him what was coming, but it had to be stated. One of us had to say it.

Face to face with something like that one is as if transfixed. Days went by. Could it be? Was it really so? At the breaking point I stood near the sofa facing him one night and told him my decision. My knees gave way under me as I said it and I collapsed on to the floor, my face in my hands.

I heard the springs of the sofa hit bottom as his weight fell upon it. Then there was a long, long silence. My eyes burned with scalding unshed tears, but I gritted my teeth, determined to go through with what I had begun.

At last I heard his voice, his own voice, not jeering or mocking, saying, "I wish you loved me."

I was in it now. The crunch of the vise, and I told myself, the truth now. Don't soft-pedal it. Be cruel.

"I don't," I told him. "And I never can again."

Someone was sobbing. It was Kent. He lifted me and carried me upstairs to my room, undressed me and put me to bed. He kissed my face a dozen times, walked out of my room and downstairs. The slam of the front door shook the house. He was gone.

Now I could sit up, bend my head on my drawn knees and cry my heart out. There were words gasped out with the tears: "Oh, I wish so too! I wish I loved him but I don't."

16

Divorce

I brought the divorce suit on the customary grounds of desertion. Kent did not defend. The court awarded me custody of the children and a small allowance for their support.

But there were two steps in a California divorce at that time. First the trial, then a year of waiting before the final decree is given. During that year, though the couple live apart, they are still married. And if they should decide to give their marriage another try, they may reunite and all is forgiven. The court awards the final decree.

That year of waiting seemed to me the worst part of all, being watched, spied upon, and argued about. Would we get back together? Or would we not?

I decided to avoid all that—simply go away somewhere and be forgotten till it was all over.

But where? I wanted mountains and sea and a golf club. And it must be cheap. Kent and I had been extravagant and we were careless about our bills, paying them when convenient. Our credit rating was "slow but good." Kent's money came in occasional chunks, such as when he had got the roadster. Now that I would have to manage alone, that must change. Responsibility for at least half the outstanding bills I must assume. My income from the Denny Estate had been a mere pittance since they had advanced so much to furnish our house.

My close friends the Van Kaathovens suggested Sea Cliff, a little hamlet on the coast fifteen miles or so south of San Francisco and close to Santa Cruz.

Van had come with his widowed mother from Holland as a small boy, had grown up and studied medicine in Philadelphia, married an American girl, Alice Henley, then they all moved on westward to Los Angeles where Van had now been practicing successfully for a number of years. They were considerably older than I but were among my dearest friends. Van was tall and handsome enough to suit even me; blond, with the ruddy coloring of his people. Alice, so sophisticated but without a trace of hardness, was all gentleness and charm. The little house at Sea Cliff was where they had established Van's old mother.

"It's the most inexpensive place imaginable," Alice said. "We go up there often to see Petite Mère. Then we'll see you too."

Of course I decided on Sea Cliff, sight unseen, and began the prodigious business of tearing myself and all my possessions loose from one place to shift to another.

I gave up my house lease. All my furniture would go into storage except what I simply had to have with me to make life tolerable for a year. Of course I must have my piano. Perhaps in that one year I could really master Chopin's "Butterfly" Etude. And the big box with my music and books and stories and typewriters. There was, too, a whole big trunk of the children's toys.

The only way to get all this heavy freight from Los Angeles to Santa Cruz would be in the hold of a steamer. I decided to ship them on the Grace Line, which ran boats up the coast. The children and I would go by train to Santa

Cruz. It would take just a couple of hours.

But first there were things to do for them. The staff of specialists, all under the eyes of a head pediatrician, had to be given explanations and dismissed. The business of straightening teeth, which O'Hara had begun, goes on for years and is expensive. That could be discontinued. An orthopedic specialist was visiting Kay regularly, attending to the exact position of his feet on his leg bones. I could watch over Kay's legs, exercises, and shoes myself.

A skin specialist, Dr. Lovejoy, advised that the tiny blue mole near the corner of O'Hara's mouth be removed while it was small. That, too, I thought could wait a year, but he advised against it. Of course I understood that specialists like these would not be in a little place like Santa Cruz.

Dr. Lovejoy said, "The smaller it is when I take it off the less chance of a scar. The way these things are done today is with liquid air. Quite painless. She won't feel a thing. It will form a scab which will drop off in a few days and that is the end of it. Better bring her in before you go away."

So that and all the other things were done, and the day came that O'Hara and Kay and I took our seats in the little train that chugged up toward San Francisco, stopping, it seemed to me, every few miles for a station.

I have told how I was considered the delicate one of the family and how little attention I paid to my illnesses. But in the past few years something different had developed which you could hardly call a mere headache. Doctors had a special name for it: migraine.

It would simply demolish me. From an active, healthy young woman I turned into a being so consumed by agony that I could only hope to pass out quickly. Doctors could not find the cause or any help for it.

Migraines were quite rare events, sort of epochal. The

way I got through them was by falling into a very deep sleep as quickly as possible. Give up doing or thinking anything, and take as many strong headache tablets as was necessary.

As O'Hara and Kay and I sat in the train that was taking us to Sea Cliff I knew that a migraine was approaching. We got off the train at the Sea Cliff station, just a little way from Santa Cruz and planned to spend the night at the Sea Cliff hotel. In the morning I would telephone a real estate agent to send a salesman with a car, and spend the day looking for a cottage. But first, somewhere, somehow, I had to find a place where I could pass out. I had the tablets with me. But I also had the children. What would I do with them while I was unconscious?

A treasure hunt! Lock them safely in the hotel room with me, then fill the entire room with a jungle of tangled spider webs of twine.

We had once done this at a Christmas party, and the children had been enthralled by it. They loved it.

I bought the two big balls of twine before we went up to the room.

When I at last took the tablets, gave myself permission to pass out and laid my body across the bed, the jungle of twine was complete above me, the children were at opposite ends of the room, each holding the end of a ball of twine. Truth is stranger than fiction. I would never have dared to put such a scene in one of my short stories.

I returned from oblivion able to carry on, and then had a good night's sleep. In the morning Mr. Hennessey came from the real estate firm to take us house hunting.

I could hardly believe my eyes when at last we found a house. It was exactly what I needed. Besides, it actually had our name on it: No. 3 Driftways.

Our place was on a large promontory overlooking the

sea. Our little lane formed the back boundary of a handsome country estate, divided from it by a white picket fence. Mr. Hennessey told me that the adjoining estate was owned by Franklyn Grace of the Grace Steamship Line.

In the days that followed, Mr. Hennessey was of the greatest assistance, first getting our telephone connected, then the utilities, then ascertaining that my piano and boxes were ready and waiting in the warehouse on the Grace Line dock. He even attended to getting the piano installed in my living room. I asked him if it would be possible for me to get a cook-general houseworker, and he later telephoned that he had located a "mother's helper," a Mrs. Ottie, who was a nice person and would do everything.

When I opened the piano and put my hands on the keys, it began to feel like home. I would not be alone there. Frédéric Chopin would be with me, and the music of all his wonderful etudes and preludes would fill 3 Driftways and roll out over the whole promontory.

It was not more than three days before a nice-looking boy of eleven or twelve presented himself at our front door and inquired if Miss Parrot was at home. This was young Frank Grace, heir presumptive of the Grace Line. His parents called a day or two after, hospitably made us free of the beautiful estate, put us up at the country club and in every possible way, welcomed us to Santa Cruz.

They were delightful people. Laura Grace and I began to do our mending together, sitting on her porch, watching the children play nearby. Frank and O'Hara became inseparable and they allowed Kay, whom they called Smitty, to tag along. He, I am sure, provided them with most of their amusement, looking for them when they disappeared, falling a victim to every trap older children can set for a younger one, but withal, was allowed to consort with them and sit down with them to barbecue feasts—roasted gophers!

O'Hara was now seven years old and still the "impossibly beautiful" child that Elma had declared her. As always, I delighted to dress her most becomingly, and that year her play suit was dark brown corduroy, a perfect foil for her dark red curls.

We had not been there long before Alice and Van Kaathoven came up to see Petite Mère, and before returning to Los Angeles drove over to see the three Driftways.

Van lifted O'Hara to his knees. "What's this?" he asked, looking at the scab which had not yet fallen off. I explained about the removed mole and he asked nothing more.

Their visit was short because it was a long drive back that day to Los Angeles and they wanted to get there before midnight.

Before breakfast the next morning, I received a long-distance call from Los Angeles. It was Dr. Lovejoy.

"Van tells me that the scab on your daughter's cheek has not fallen off yet."

"No. It hasn't. There's just a little lump."

"Well, now here's what you must do."

He gave me the name and address of a Dr. Guthrie, the best dermatologist in San Francisco.

"He'll attend to it. Don't delay. Go tomorrow if you can. The longer that scab stays on the more chance of its leaving a scar."

As I hung up the receiver I stood for a moment, suddenly anxious. Could anything be the matter? One heard things about moles. But Dr. Lovejoy's voice had held no trace of anxiety. Don't imagine things. Then I started mentally counting my money, for it was nearing the end of the month and I was low on cash.

However, the trip ought not to cost much. Return tickets there and back, a taxi to the doctor's office, another back to the station and a snack lunch at the drugstore.

O'Hara could wear her black and white check coat, white felt hat with a wide brim rolled up and back.

We caught the morning train.

17

The Blue Mole

D r. Guthrie's offices were on the tenth floor. Going up in the elevator O'Hara squeezed into one corner and watched the operator as he swung the lever back and forth to open and close the doors at the various stops, the cables overhead smoothly obeying the same mysterious orders.

Every eye was on O'Hara. People stared at her, smiling, fascinated as if at a bright exotic flower or a jeweled butterfly. The elevator door opened and O'Hara and I walked down a long corridor toward the doctor's office. At last we reached a door which had his name on it. The small reception room was empty and we sat down to wait. Soon a nurse came in, saying, "Dr. Guthrie will see you now, Mrs. Parrot."

Dr. Guthrie was a tall man, very well dressed and with an air of brisk command about him. His spectacles had an almost invisible frame, and from behind these his light blue eyes were cold and piercing.

I took off O'Hara's hat and coat and told the story of her mole. Long before I finished he had drawn her to the strong light by the window, looked a moment at the mole, then began feeling under her jaw. He asked me if she had any lumps anywhere on her body and I said no, there were none.

Then he let go of her, stood up and removed his spectacles. He began to polish them, staring out the window. My heart began to pound.

I was almost relieved when he said he would like to consult with another dermatologist who had an office in the same building, a Dr. Harrison. I consented immediately.

Presently Dr. Harrison entered, was introduced and I retold the story of the mole.

Dr. Harrison did just what Dr. Guthrie had done, then the two men looked at each other.

When I tried to speak my voice shook. "Will you please tell me what the matter is?" I stammered.

They told me. The scab on O'Hara's cheek was a sarcoma, a malignant growth. If cells from this tumor had already reached other parts of her body, there was little hope. If not, she had a chance.

Dr. Guthrie said, "But surgery must be performed immediately."

"If she was my child," Dr. Harrison added, "I'd have that out today."

I answered almost angrily, "That's what I came here for—to have it taken off."

"Not off, but out," Dr. Guthrie replied. "The cheek must be removed. Just the tip of the growth shows."

Dr. Guthrie got a book out of a wall case, opened it to a chapter headed "Sarcoma," and showed me a colored picture.

My head swam and I had to sit down. I didn't say another word, but sat listening as they told me I really had no choice, the child's life was in danger. They discussed with each other who the surgeon should be and decided on a Dr. Prentiss. Several telephone calls were made: to Dr.

Prentiss, the hospital, again to Dr. Prentiss.

While all this was going on O'Hara stood at the window, looking down at the traffic many flights below, where cable cars and automobiles and people looked like ants. Her breath fogged the glass. She rubbed it off and peered again.

Before I left the office I had given my consent. The operation would be at two thirty that afternoon.

In the street we walked along slowly. I didn't know where I was. I knew I had consented to surgery but I didn't believe the diagnosis—not any of it. Such things couldn't be true. The conviction that it was true hit me like a hard physical blow and I came to a sudden stop. Then came relief, because it couldn't really be true; it was silly to believe it; it was like a nightmare. I moved forward again. Again the conviction. Belief and disbelief came like regular pulsations while my mind struggled to accept the truth and grapple with it. I had a decision to make and not much time to make it in: take her to the hospital where they would cut off that firm rounded cheek, color of cream and roses, or let her be devoured by those malignant cells.

"Mummy, I'm hungry," said O'Hara. "Isn't it lunchtime yet?"

"What would you like for lunch?"

"Cold chicken, if I may eat it with my fingers."

"You may."

O'Hara added hastily, "And ice cream and chocolate sauce for dessert."

"All right."

"Oh, goody!" She gave a little skip. "Mummy, where are we going? You walk as if you didn't know."

We were approaching the St. Francis Hotel, where I frequently lunched when I was in San Francisco. Automatically I turned in.

That is how I happened to meet Peter Bristol on that fateful day. *Doctor* Bristol, with whom I had played many a game of golf when he was visiting in Los Angeles.

Until the three of us had taken our seats at a table and given our orders, I hid my terror. Then I told Peter the whole story. My only hope was that those two doctors might be wrong. Peter listened to me very gravely.

"Do they know, Peter? Could they be wrong about it?"

"They know. And if they say it's a sarcoma, it is. But they're not the final authority on this sort of case. That would be Meredith Ayres. I wonder—" He stopped talking and suddenly pushed his chair back. "I wonder if Dr. Ayres could see you. I'll ring his office."

When he returned, a glance at his face showed me he had been successful.

"We'll walk," he said. "He's only a couple of blocks away."

O'Hara licked her spoon one last time and I put on her things.

Peter, evidently a privileged character, took us to the back door of Dr. Ayres's suite, which instantly opened to admit us. We sat down to wait.

Presently Dr. Ayres came in. Peter introduced us, then said to me, "I'll leave you now. Dr. Ayres will give you the best advice to be had." We clasped hands.

The door closed behind him and I turned to Dr. Ayres. Our eyes met and he smiled. He was a much older man with a strong and authoritative face; a face I could trust. I felt a pang of hope.

"This is the little girl," he said. "Dr. Bristol has told me all about it."

There was a repetition of Dr. Guthrie's examination of O'Hara, but no haste about it. The nurse came in and offered O'Hara a tiny toy monkey to play with. The doctor went away to telephone, came back and sat studying her, watching her as if the solution to the problem was right there in her cheek.

He left the room again to telephone and this time was gone quite a long while. I had a sudden conviction he had made up his mind to something and I was on my feet, standing nervously behind a chair when he returned.

"There will be no operation this afternoon. I have countermanded it."

I clutched the back of the chair and leaned over it, weakened by the wave of relief. I closed my eyes; his voice, continuing in even tones, came from a distance and suddenly the nurse was beside me, holding me, pushing the chair around for me to sit on.

"There are other ways of dealing with such tumors than extensive excision," he was saying.

Extensive excision. That meant, as they had said, taking off the cheek.

"Of course I told Dr. Guthrie you had come to me," he continued.

The nurse brought O'Hara's hat and coat and began to put them on her while I stood up.

Dr. Ayres got up more slowly.

"You're going over to see Dr. Foster now."

O'Hara laughed and counted them off on her fingers. "That's six, Mummy! My mole has had six doctors!"

Dr. Ayres sent us on our way in his own limousine. Presently we were in Dr. Foster's office and found both him and the nurse ready and waiting for us. The doctor, attired in his white surgeon's coat, was seated on a high stool. The nurse removed O'Hara's things, slipped over her a long white gown and lifted her to a stool facing the doctor.

O'Hara watched with growing alarm at these preparations, and gave a questioning look at the doctor. He showed her the small foot-long metal rod he held.

"I'm going to take your mole off with this."

"Will it hurt?" she asked.

"You won't even feel it, because I'll give you a needle first, a hypo. You've had needles, haven't you?"

"I've been vaccinated," she replied.

I held up a fifty-cent piece. "See this? I'll give it to you if you sit still and don't make a fuss about the hypo."

O'Hara screwed up her face and shut her eyes and demanded, "Will there be a scar?"

"Not any more than a dimple," Dr. Foster promised. "Right at the corner of your mouth where a dimple ought to be."

The fifty-cent piece and dimple tipped the scales and the nurse plugged in the wire, which was attached to the end of the little poker. It began to glow pink as the doctor, almost painlessly, administered the hypodermic.

After that O'Hara felt no more pain. Between tears and laughter she boasted, "I was brave, wasn't I, Mummy?" and pocketed the fifty-cent piece. The metal poker was white hot.

"Now," said the doctor, "we'll get that mole off. Shut your eyes again and sit still."

I watched the rod touch the mole, and press in. The flesh sizzled. I could have counted to five before the doctor withdrew it.

It was over. A small dressing—a patch of gauze—was applied, held on the cheek with two little strips of adhesive. While the nurse put on O'Hara's coat and hat, I had a word with the doctor.

"Was it malignant?"

"There's no way of telling without doing a biopsy. But if it wasn't yet, it would have been. In any case this cauterization would have been the thing to do."

We made the five o'clock train back to Santa Cruz. Mrs. Ottie had waited supper for us.

18

"Wind Harp"

The rest of my year of exile passed without earthshaking events, indeed with considerable pleasure, although I fretted at the delay in getting on with my writing career.

If a woman has failed at the career of wife and homemaker, she must have another worthwhile career and take it seriously. Up till now my attitude toward writing had been that of a dilettante. Plans, urges, and a great deal of determination were stirring in me and I wished I could talk them over with Fanny.

She had spent a weekend with me once at 3 Driftways and Mrs. Ottie had outdone herself with a delicious fish dinner, but that hardly gave us time to do more than catch up with today before it was tomorrow and she was gone.

I missed the rest of my Los Angeles friends, too, and the Sunday mixed foursomes at the club. I wished that I was home.

At last came the day when the final divorce decree was

awarded. I was no longer a wife, Kent was no longer a husband.

The day after the final decree was awarded, Kent married Virginia Pierce, a pretty young divorcee with whom the Frasers were good friends. (That marriage was to last just one year.)

Upon moving back to Los Angeles we were met at the station by the Macfarlands, whom the children called Uncle Dan and Aunty Lou. They had been close neighbors of ours, and they took us to their house for a sumptuous dinner—turkey and candles and a fancy dessert—a real celebration, even if it was for nothing but our homecoming. And we were to stay with them until we had found a house.

Fanny and I had a session at her house the next day. She told me there would be the usual mixed foursomes the coming Sunday afternoon, and when she had told A. D. S. Johnston I would be home, he had asked her to get him a date with me. He and I together had already won many of those little silver cups.

Soon, all was as it had been before.

At about this time I acquired a possession which I was to cherish all my life. My own piano. Up to this time my piano had been rented, some good, some bad. I was convinced that in the long run it would be more economical to own one rather than continue to rent, and I haunted the music shops. Up on the second floor of the biggest music store in Los Angeles, where the pianos were, I would ask the salesmen to leave me alone and let me try them. And so I experimented, wondering if I would have judgment enough, experience enough, to make a good selection.

The salesmen got to know me. They had, of course, secondhand pianos too, or knew of them, and that is what I hoped to come upon: a parlor or even a grand piano which had been used in a school or church and now was no longer wanted. And that is what, eventually, I was lucky enough to find.

My piano had originally been chosen out of dozens of others by the great Godofsky for a pupil who was, beyond a doubt, a genius. The pupil practiced on it for a year, then was sent to Paris by a rich patron to finish his education there.

The piano had stood silent in his empty room until the father of the boy decided to sell it.

One of the piano salesmen who had noticed my preoccupation with pianos told me about it and the fact that it was in a little house that had no telephone. He gave me the address. Mr. Berle, the father of the genius, was apologetic about the idea of selling his son's piano. He was a typesetter at the *Los Angeles Times*, and had many other children to support. "He won't need it when he comes back because then he will be famous and they will *pay him* to play on their instruments.

"It is as good as new, it has been played on for just one year, but it is now secondhand. Mr. Godofsky got it for a discount price because he is Godofsky. I can let you have it for half of what he paid for it."

A number of children had crowded into the room behind us and stood listening and staring at me. Mr. Berle took a key from his pocket and opened the instrument. It was a double-B Mason and Hamlin concert grand. I sat down on the bench.

"Any other geniuses?" I asked him.

He looked at the children affectionately. "No. They are just common children. From them I have happiness."

I played on the piano for a few minutes. The wonderful sounds rang through the empty room, stealing my senses away.

There was never any doubt that this was the piano I wanted.

My interest in music had never flagged. It was probably, I thought, my true vocation, and writing merely an avocation—I played every day and it amounted to a good many hours, though I never called it practicing. But when the inspiration for a story seized me, I would decide it was the other way around, and writing was my vocation.

Long before I moved to California, a musician named Vernon Spencer had established himself there. Born in England, he had been educated at the Leipzig Conservatory of Music before coming to the United States to live.

He was a piano virtuoso and gave many recitals when he first reached Los Angeles, married and settled down. He began to give piano lessons too. His energy was inexhaustible. Eventually he added lecturing to his labor. He was an excellent talker and never seemed to run out of things to say about music. The diploma from the Leipzig Conservatory helped him to obtain a lecturing job at the university.

When I first met him he was late middle-aged, already known throughout town as "The Master." It was as a teacher that his genius had flowered. He took only students who were aiming at a concert career and capable of getting there.

In his big house near Los Feliz Boulevard, his music room held not one but two concert grand pianos, standing close together, side by side. The student, coming with a well-prepared lesson, sat at the right-hand piano, Mr. Spencer at the left. Mr. Spencer, his eyes glued to the notes, would lean forward, ready to come in with a shout, or a few crashing chords at just the right moment to galvanize the pupil into outdoing himself.

There was nothing about music which he did not know—harmony and composition, counterpoint, its past history, all the music which had been written, present composers, all the great publishing houses. He was not only a musicologist, but one whose fame had spread across the continent, so that he had become an authority, listed in *Who's Who*.

I have the nose of a hound for a good teacher and can catch the whiff of a bad one at the first glance—the bigotry, or arrogance or bluff. I love to be taught. What is there better in life? When a friend who had been listening to me playing some of my compositions said, "Why don't you take a lot of these to this Vernon Spencer? He might be able to figure out why you can't get them published," I gave it serious consideration.

It was true none of my songs had been published, though when I sent a song to one publisher I had got a very nice note back: "This is musical and has charm. You should study." This puzzled me. What more could it need if it was musical and had charm? So much that was published had not.

At this time Mr. Spencer had a second wife, Ruth, a lovely young girl to sit at his feet and adore him, and my friend was acquainted with her, so all was arranged. My ears still tingle when I remember his praise and excitement.

"What talent! How beautiful! Every one a perfect little gem, capable of being developed into larger forms."

He examined every one, accompanying the music with a running commentary of strange sounds, half exclamation, half grunts, sometimes going back to repeat one, or a small section of one over and over. At last he was through, pushed himself away from the piano and took off his glasses.

At last he rendered his verdict. "In four years I can teach you all that can be taught about music. You have the gift of melody. When you know how to compose you can

become at least as distinguished a composer as Chaminade."

I was thrilled beyond measure by such a prospect—
were not all the girls buying and practicing pieces by
Chaminade? "The Scarf Dance," "The Flatterer." I drew a
few more sheets of music out of my case. These were the
sketches I had made so many years ago, illustrating our
happy days at Deercreek.

"I've sent these to several publishers but they always
send them back."

He glanced at them briefly. I was ashamed of the
writing. Nearly all of my piano playing was by ear and I
had shunned the dry labor of studying how the notes were
set on the sheets.

He gave his head a little shake and handed them back
to me. "They are not edited," he said. "No publisher
would buy them. No one could read them."

Our lessons began, two a week. I went through his
textbooks, doing all the exercises so easily and quickly he
said that he was able to give me five lessons in every visit.
His wife and I became good friends and I was much at their
house.

One day he edited the Deercreek pieces for me, saying
it would take him a half hour, but to teach me how to do it
would take a year. I watched him, fascinated by the long
swooping slurs of his pencil, the dots or small horizontal
bars over certain notes, the abbreviation "Ped." at certain
points under the staff, followed at the exact, correct
distance by a star.

"But people know how to pedal," I protested.

"You'd be surprised. Count on their knowing
nothing. It's *your* job." Now came the expression marks
which he called the dynamics.

When it was done it looked like no manuscript that
had ever come from my pen before. It was sent to Theodore
Presser of Philadelphia and was accepted. They published

before a year had passed. It was gotten up very artistically and had a good sale. It kept on selling and every so often, even after all these years, I meet someone who has heard it recently at a recital.

The lessons added zest to my already zestful life. Unfortunately they had to be stopped when Kay fell ill with diphtheria. My house was taken in charge by nurses from the health department. I would nurse him myself, I declared. Then I must be quarantined with him they told me. Sterilized sheets divided the space we would occupy from the rest of the household.

I saw to it that my piano was quarantined with Kay and me, and during those weary and anxious weeks I composed three pieces—"Idle Moments," "Silver Heels," and "Novelette in G." I put into them all the new things I had learned from Mr. Spencer, and took them to him as soon as Kay was recovered. These too were accepted and published by Presser.

Then I did a piece of gay nonsense which I had a lot of fun with and called it "Bagatelle." When I took that to Mr. Spencer and he played it, he exclaimed, "You savage! You savage," and crossed the room to throw open the door to the anteroom where several students sat waiting for their lessons, exclaiming, "Listen to this composition! She has broken every rule, and justified it by creating an immensely dramatic effect!"

Mr. Spencer never lost interest in me and was always anxious to see anything I wrote. He kept urging me to write first- and second-degree piano pieces, saying that established composers would not bother with them, there was practically nothing on the market for beginners. And I did as he told me and wrote more of them. But I improvised a great deal at the piano, and one day was playing music that suddenly made me stop playing and cover my face with my hands, trembling all over. This music became the two alternating themes of "Wind Harp."

ˈI let it grow into a piece several pages long but could not work much at it because it put me to bed with shock and wonder. I did not know what it was.

When I played it for Mr. Spencer it had the same effect upon him. He played the two themes over again and again, muttering, "However did you get them?"

Then he went to the door of his anteroom and dismissed the students that were there, waiting for lessons, and came back to the piano again. Again the two themes, and the muttering.

Then he looked at me. "This is a concert etude in the style of Chopin. If you can properly develop these themes it will be a very big piece. Have you any idea what they express? *Love.* Pure burning love . . . What do you know about love . . . ?"

He went to a little couch, sat down and drew me down beside him. "I can't teach today. Forgive me if I skip your lesson."

Then he poured out his life story: his unhappy first marriage; his disappointment in his four children; his dismay when they proved, one by one, to have no musical awareness. Absolutely tone deaf—all of them.

Then he went further back to his childhood and a life of near poverty in a country town near London. Fed, educated, but refused a pair of long trousers when he was fourteen because they would cost fifteen dollars and his short ones were still in good shape. The occasion occurred when a new organist was needed for the local church. Applicants had to present themselves for auditions. Vernon was sure he could win the post and he did. But he won it in short pants and was ashamed. His father said that since he was small for his age it looked better anyway.

Walking home from choir rehearsal one night, he noticed through an uncurtained upper window, a young woman undressing for the night, and paused. Her dress was off. Vernon stopped, watching, while she turned her back

Mary O'Hara as a child.

Grandma May.

Mary with sisters, Bess and Elma, 1898.

As a young woman.

Papa Alsop.

Mary's brother Reese.

Kent Parrot.

Mary O'Hara writing continuity scripts at the studio.

George Burnell.

O'Hara Parrot.

Helge Sture-Vasa and Mary, the summer of 1945.

Mary O'Hara, Remount Ranch.

Mary's son, Kent, and his new bride, Deirdre, 1948.

Tyrawley.

Mary in her library.

and went into the closet to hang it up. When she came out she was in long white petticoat and corset cover. She began to untie the strings that tied the petticoat around her waist.

There was a telegraph pole near her window and Vernon climbed the pole so he could get a better view. Down came the petticoat and off went the corset cover. There she was in white corsets that reached from her hips nearly to her armpits. From the lower edge elastic supporters attached themselves to long black stockings.

Then came the struggle with the corsets. Vernon watched her bend and wriggle till the clasps opened and, drawing a deep breath of relief, she drew them off and threw them over the back of a chair, and removed her stockings.

But she was still well-covered. A chemise of sheer white nainsook was tucked into a pair of white linen drawers of knee length, trimmed at the bottom with lace. These too fastened with a string. She undid it. They fell to the floor and she stepped out of them, and pulled the chemise over her head. She stood naked. Her hands went to her head and drew out a number of large hairpins. Masses of fair hair rolled down her back. She picked up her brush and began to brush it with long swinging strokes.

So the little boy became a man, clinging desperately to the pole as wave after wave of sensation rolled through him.

While Mr. Spencer had described the episode the afternoon had passed and the light waned.

He finished and there was a long silence. Then came the final cadence on a tired sigh of reminiscence. "So that's how I learned about love."

"Love?" I asked.

"Oh, yes. Love. I was mad for her."

We were silent again. The room was almost dark. Then, as if he had an afterthought, he thrust out his right foot and pulled up the trouser leg. I saw the cause of his slight limp to which I was so accustomed that I no longer noticed. He had a club foot.

He readjusted the trouser leg.

Then, in a bright changed voice, he apologized. "I know you won't mind. I just had to tell you. Tell you everything. I feel much better."

He patted my cheek, got up, and turned the lights on.

19

George Edwin Burnell

I was obliged now to reverse again my opinion that writing was my true vocation and music a mere avocation. A man like Vernon Spencer knew what he was talking about. The possibility of ever becoming the equal of Chaminade overwhelmed me and I was eager to begin again the biweekly lessons which Spencer had said would be necessary.

But there came into my life at that time something which I can only call miraculous. Yes. I believe in miracles. In a large, general way I believe everyone does—believes in Someone or Something we call God, who made the world and people and ongoing events and art and beauty and made it all out of Himself—or nothing.

But there were small special kinds of miracles which He sometimes performed, as if He condescended to enter the world He had made Himself, and take part in the game, as when a great hand in the Bible came down out of the sky and wrote a warning upon a wall. Or when Meshach, Shadrach, and Abednego were thrown into the burning fiery furnace, and He entered the furnace and stood beside them and none of them were burned.

What happened was this. I went with a friend to hear a lecture on the *Upanishads* given by a man whose name was George Edwin Burnell. The moment I heard his voice, I recognized that here was the voice, the mind that had spoken the words "cosmic sadness" and had somehow transmitted them to me fifteen years before in Brooklyn, New York. After the lecture, he mingled with his audience and there was general conversation. I asked him if he had ever known Jack London.

Mr. Burnell answered that he had. "Jack London was a student of mine. He lived in my house for two years before he was married."

Mr. Burnell was a big, impressive-looking man about sixty-five, thickset, with swarthy skin like a Hindu and dark burning eyes. He reminded me of Savonarola, the fifteenth-century monk who thundered denunciations at the corrupt Medicis. Altogether, he looked foreign, but I had heard that his parents were Irish, born in this country.

I went to more of his lectures and got to know his entire family; his wife, married daughter, Genevieve, and fourteen-year-old grandson. The Burnells lived in an old-fashioned neighborhood of Los Angeles in a house arranged like a small school. It was large enough to accommodate the assistants and male and female secretaries and groups of devotees who had attached themselves permanently to the center. Lectures were given downstairs where the rooms could be thrown into each other. Upstairs, Mr. Burnell gave private lessons in his own room and Mrs. Burnell healing treatments in hers.

There are some people who, from birth onward, are dedicated to religion. To learn, to understand the relationship between God and man, to acquire the powers which accompany such understanding, then to pass on to others what they have gained for themselves—these are the qualities of the great teachers, the sages, the avatars.

I was sure that Mr. Burnell was one of these and I was stunned to think that Fate had led me to sit at the feet of one of the great teachers. Possibly we were already linked. Possibly he had drawn me to him by those two words, "cosmic sadness," had thrown them, like a boomerang, around my mind to bring me to him.

It was expected that I would fall in line behind the other devotees, come to all the lectures, haunt the Burnell house, and make this instruction the center of my life. But I could not do this. I was by nature independent and could not let anyone, not even Mr. Burnell, just pick me up and put me in his vest pocket. Besides, I was already committed to a writing career and the endless amount of work that preparation for it requires.

When he became aware of this, he exerted a little pressure, saying that worldly ambitions are apt to be disappointing. Moreover, he added, when a student becomes a candidate for illumination, he simply abandons such things, forgets them, pushes them away.

When arguments had no effect upon me, there was a truce in our tug-of-war, though he said to me once, smiling, "I think you are resisting me." I felt he wanted to take possession of me for some purpose, perhaps to be one of his assistants.

Suddenly his attitude changed, all pressure, all arguments ceased. He asked me to play a game of golf with him.

Now I had the chance I had been waiting for and I asked him about cosmic sadness. He took it lightly. It amused him and I was puzzled.

"But it's terribly important! It's a miracle. Those two words are what led me to you."

"Yes," he agreed, "you tracked them to their lair, didn't you?"

I was still baffled. "Tracked them? From Brooklyn,

New York to Los Angeles? And taking fifteen years to do it?"

We were walking from the ninth green to the next tee.

Mr. Burnell explained. "Space and time are hypothetical. Invented structures of the human mind upon which to build more fantasies."

Though his lectures drew freely from East Indian mysticism, they were not limited to that, or, indeed to any established religion. They were pure Burnellian. Parables, metaphors, always ambiguous, the simplest statement a paradox.

We hit our next tee shots and walked after our balls.

"The first thing for a student to acquire is the perception of nothingness."

The Bible said, "And the firmament shall be rolled up like a scroll."

A scroll. A paper with a story written on it. How many I had thrown into the wastebasket, always with a sense of disentanglement and relief.

So we talked, played our games of golf, went to the movies together, sometimes the theater, or just took long drives in his car. This casual, friendly relationship suited me. I saw that I was to be his playmate, the companion of his hours of relaxation.

Mr. Burnell could not open his mouth without instructing. Insights, new points of view were showered upon me. Childish complexes were stripped from me. I was actually getting many hours of private instruction with this man whom dozens of people tried unavailingly to see. For me it was the pouring out of a cornucopia of precious knowledge.

Of course, I was already familiar with the basic tenets of Hindu mysticism that he was preaching, "All is Mind," and recognized many familiar quotations: "He being one, wished to be many"; "The flight of the alone to the alone."

I had written my Papa about all this, but he scoffed at it. "Run into that table and when the corner collides with your hip you'll know whether or not matter is real," he had written.

But such tenets were spreading, especially in California. Under the general term New Thought, there came into being a host of cults: Unity, Mental Science, Theosophy, the Immanual Movement.

I had questions to ask Mr. Burnell which had long been unanswered, such as my puzzlement over the second person of the Trinity. "Why do we always have to say at the end of our prayers, through Jesus Christ our Lord?"

He turned and gave me a very direct look, harsh and penetrating, "Because He rules all. He is our protection against any danger. *Remember* that!" For once he spoke unambiguously and in plain English, and I was frightened a little.

If I was ill he came to see me, accompanied by Mrs. Burnell or his secretary, Lucille. He seemed concerned about me. I was accustomed to frequent attacks of bronchitis and laryngitis. At night I had to sit upright, my head down on a pillow across my knees to get any respite from the violent coughing spells which seemed as if they would tear me apart. So I made light of my illnesses to Mr. Burnell, telling him, laughingly, that I started at four with diphtheria that almost killed me.

"So they tried to do away with you before you even got started?"

I wondered who "they" were—he referred to "them" quite often and always with an altered expression. Sages—wise men—could see on other levels than the earthly level I knew.

It seemed to me that Mr. Burnell knew something about me which I did not know myself. He thought I was in danger, not in danger as every young woman is in danger who has repudiated her parents, their advice and shelter, and the community in which she grew up, but a danger more specific than that. And he felt an obligation to protect me.

This feeling persisted in me. What was it he knew about me? Our friendship deepened.

I went to him one day when I was in terrible trouble and burst into tears as Lucille shut the door behind me. I was consumed with such violent weeping that it choked me and I could not speak a word. I cried for six hours, hearing nothing of what Mr. Burnell, from time to time, said. He canceled all his other engagements. I was torn to pieces as I watched the crumbling away of my future life. It took the whole day.

At last the room was quiet. I was calmly wiping my eyes when Mr. Burnell said, "Now you've got through that. You'll never have to go through it again. I promise you."

To take a student out of whatever trap of materialism he was caught in, shake him loose, give him new insights, this is what he could do.

I learned new techniques of dealing with illness or trouble. You did not just pray, asking for divine help, you "Treated" the situation yourself. This was done by affirmation and denial. You affirmed the allness and goodness of God. You denied the possibility that anything could alter or spoil or cover the perfection of God's perfect creation.

All this is done with words.

I cannot say that one's troubles simply evaporate the moment one knows that they are nothing, but there were many healings and many deliverances.

In those days it was considered slightly disgraceful to be poor, as if a God would be niggardly with his children. There was as much money available as was needed. Right thinking would pay your bills as well as heal your body. Millions of Christian Scientists had been "demonstrating" this for years.

The Burnells owned a summer place right on the
ocean at Redondo Beach, as well as a beautiful landed estate
at Arcadia in the hills above Pasadena. This was the last
property acquired, an estate suitable to a millionaire, and
Mr. Burnell was very proud of it. He liked to lecture there
on Sundays. People would drive out in their cars and the
children would wander around out of doors during the
lecture.

We had an interesting talk about dreams. He gave
them great importance. Not only the dreams described in
the Bible but the modern talk about Freud's theories. I had
nothing to contribute as, to my great annoyance, I did not
dream at all. Mr. Burnell was surprised when I told him
this, then his look changed to one of puzzled calculation as
if something hidden were to be disclosed.

"That is," I explained, "not real nighttime dreams.
Only daydreams. Plenty of those. Pipe dreams."

"But you mustn't do that," he said sharply. "You
must stop it."

"Easier said than done," was my laughing rejoinder.
"It is a lifetime habit."

Mr. Burnell's head moved sharply.

It was as if he gave an order.

From that moment on my dreaming habits were
reversed. My daydreaming stopped and my nights were
filled with a fantasmagoria of wild experiences, as if he had
reached into the deepest caverns of my psyche and pressed a
switch which turned the flood of my thoughts into a new
direction.

Gradually my fantastic dreams quieted down. They
became serene, even beautiful, but different from any I had
ever had before. I was simply gazing out—traveling around
in a country I had never seen before.

Finally I had a dream I felt was significant, like the
Bible dreams. I have never forgotten it though sixty years
have passed. From some high point I was looking at the

interior of a huge glass dome. It was symmetrical, empty, silent, lit with a pale silvery gray translucence. Far, far away in the distance a single motionless figure stood on the center of the gray stone floor, wearing a dress of tight dark gray wrapping.

The dream must have had some significance. I have never seen anything like it. Who could that silent, motionless watcher have been? Mr. Burnell himself? I was not to discover.

I had more other-worldly and beautiful dreams, then one so terrible that it is painful to write about it. Something was in my room, someone monstrous like an oversized man. He hurled himself across the room at me with the force of a catapult and fell upon me. He tore at my tongue, trying to pull it out by the roots, and then flipped me over and laid an arm like an iron crowbar across my back, and bent my legs up. My bones cracked. I remembered what Mr. Burnell had said and screamed, "Jesus Christ!"

The monster vanished. My room was empty and quiet. There was not a mark on me so it must all have been a dream but I cannot believe it. It was a murderous attack upon me by one of those evil things that roam the hinterlands of our thought.

After that I could never say again that I was not acquainted with the second person of the Trinity. In my thankfulness I was humbled and shamed, and on my knees.

Mr. Burnell's prophecies to the effect that I would probably be disappointed in my worldly ambitions, my search after fame, would not prove to be correct. Everyone was supposed to prosper under the Burnell instruction, but in my case he disclaimed all credit, insisting I would have done just as well without him. I think he was glad of it and enjoyed hearing about it.

What would prove a strain on our relationship was my

second marriage, my "happy marriage," for he and my future husband disliked each other on sight—though dislike is perhaps the wrong word. Dislike would be contrary to Mr. Burnell's calling. Since those who came to Mr. Burnell were expected to stay with him, he looked with disfavor on the man who intended to take me away with him to another part of the country.

Mr. Burnell said, "This is not in my plan."

Mr. Burnell's life had long since shaped itself in a regular pattern of lectures, movement from Los Angeles, to Redondo, to Arcadia according to the season with one big birthday party every year, and never varied.

Our association was really at an end in spite of the fact that it was Mr. Burnell who had changed me as no one else ever had, a change like turning a glove inside out, a sort of second birth, a conversion. The nurse I and my siblings had had in Brooklyn as little children saw us when we were middle-aged and had an opportunity to size us up. She said we were the same—all except Mary. I was different. I had been changed.

And so Mr. Burnell led me, from first to last, with patience and forbearance, with wisdom, goodness, and indulgence: from the first, which was the cosmic sadness, to the last, which was a visit I paid to him at Arcadia before I went abroad.

To arrange a visit to Mr. Burnell at this time was quite complicated because he was old now, and gave no more private lessons. I got an appointment when Lucille had carried my message to him—that I was going abroad and just wanted to say good-bye. As she ushered me into his study she said in a low voice, "Just a few minutes now."

I had often seen the large second-story room which he inhabited at Arcadia. It jutted out from the house with tall windows on three sides, flooding the upper part of the room with light. To walk into it was to walk into a veritable forest of bookcases of uniform size, about four feet wide and the height of a man. They jutted in all directions and were pushed back to leave a cleared space in the center. Mr. Burnell was sitting there in his big armchair with a great tome open on his knees. My heart hurt as I saw how old and frail he looked. His hair was pure silver.

I chatted as I approached, telling him I was going abroad, promising not to visit with him more than a minute. He glanced up at me but did not lift his head. If his conventional responses were words, I do not remember them. Both his hands lay upon the arms of his chair and they did not move.

I stood close by him. How could I thank him? Ask his forgiveness? Tell him that I loved him? I lifted one of his hands, held it in both of mine and laid it against my cheek. It was a plea for forgiveness if ever I had been lacking in veneration for him, if I had been mulish and stubborn, always wanting my own willful way.

At last he spoke, choosing just the words to voice his approval of me, really a benediction: "Pretty pink dress."

It was a new dress I was wearing that day, a skirt and jacket of soft pleated silk, with a small black velvet collar.

He said it again as Lucille opened the door and spoke my name. "Pretty pink dress."

So I knew he had forgiven me.

I laid his hand down and left the room.

I never saw him again, for he died soon after that visit and was followed within six months by Mrs. Burnell. I returned from abroad to an atmosphere of emptiness and grief.

The fire had gone out, but not for me. I felt his presence—not that of a dying man, but again vigorous and energetic. And very close to me.

This has not diminished. In moments of crisis, one clings to a friend. If the friend is absent, the tentacle of thought reaches out, searching even the ranks of the dead. In such moments it is always Mr. Burnell whom I find and with whom I have long imaginary conversations. I ask questions about things that still puzzle me. I invent his answers drawing from memories of things I recall his having said when he was still alive.

For instance, he once said, in a way that was almost surly, "I always knew you'd get it."

What did that mean, unless, possibly, that if everything mortal mind conceives of is the same as nothing, then that leaves only what is eternal and changeless and indestructible.

I also recalled that he said, once, when I had asked for something, "I will put your little candle on the table and shove it forward when the great conflagration comes—if I can remember it."

I have nothing more to ask of him nowadays, but when I think of him, his presence is as strong as ever.

He keeps the rendezvous.

PART THREE

20

Career Woman

When I lived in Los Angeles in the silent film days, to live in or near Hollywood was like residing near a court.

The whole world was interested in movies and the people who made them. Americans, having no royalty, bequeathed the term and trappings on their great movie stars and directors.

There were careers of many different kinds in Hollywood open to women. The one I was interested in was writing. My head was full of stories suitable for the screen.

I knew the four big motion picture companies—Paramount, Warner Brothers, Metro, and Universal—straddled the country, having their production studios in Hollywood and the power, the final authority, in New York. New York bought the story material which Hollywood had to make into pictures, and bought only works which had already achieved a big reputation: Broadway hit plays and best-selling books.

This system did not work smoothly. Sometimes Hollywood received stuff which simply could not be photographed. One can imagine the dismay of the production manager who read Maeterlink's famous play and screamed, "The leading man is a bird!"

Newspaper editorials urged the country's novelists to write directly for the screen. Many less ambitious writers who had seen plenty of train wrecks and tidal waves on the screen were sure they could do as well. And so many so-called originals were mailed to the studios. But it proved dangerous. The studios were unscrupulous about plagiarizing or pirating anything they wanted. It was not safe.

I decided I would take my stories in myself—get an appointment with the head of the scenario department, talk to him about his stars, write directly for one of the stars. But my name was not known. So far I had sold nothing. There were hordes of people, would-be writers, trying to get into those studios. Sometimes I drove past them slowly, thinking what it would be like to be one of the people who could go in and out.

The premises, as large as a city block, enclosing a number of stages, were surrounded by impassable barriers with entrances only here and there, closely guarded. If the guard knew you, or you had a pass with a certain signature, he nodded and you went in. Otherwise you did not.

The ones going in and out were the stars (in big limousines), the extras, the directors, writers, continuity writers, title and treatment writers, technical men, editors, cutters, prop boys, script girls, wardrobe women, hairdressers.

What I needed, I thought, was a stroke of luck. No one ever got anywhere without a bit of luck to help them. I never thought I'd get it at the golf club.

Seldom did any of the moving-picture people play golf at the L.A. Country Club. But young Dick Hyland belonged to the club. His uncle was a governor, and he himself was a director at Metro. He was between pictures, and asked me for a game.

Dick was in a bad humor. The picture he had just finished was not a success—not exactly a flop, but not ready to release. Now he and his production head were fighting about the length, what scenes to cut, what to leave in.

I sympathized with his troubles, and before our round ended had a chance to tell him about "Love Sickness." He thought the title a knockout and I asked if he would read it. He promised to take it home with him and, if he liked it, take it to Joe Blakeman, who was the head of the scenario department.

"He's the only one who could buy it. But there's never much chance for an original."

"Love Sickness" went into Metro in Dick Hyland's coat pocket, and my hopes were high.

Two days later he was on the telephone. "Sorry, but Joe can't use your story. Not a good part for his star. But he was bowled over by your dialogue."

"Dialogue? I didn't do any special dialogue."

"Your story's full of it. Corcoran read it too. Corcoran's been doctoring a sick picture. A new set of titles, brilliant titles, he feels, might help."

These were the days of the silent films. Whenever words were necessary to get the sense over to the audience they would appear on the screen written in small type, telling the audience of the passing of time, of subtle things impossible to photograph.

"Brilliant titles?" I wondered.

"Corcoran wants to know if you'll take a job in the cutting room."

I knew that every production unit had a gang of boys who took physical charge of the heavy reels of film when all the shooting had been done. They numbered the shots, with the continuity writer's script to go by. Then they took it back to the cutting room, cutting it and splicing it where necessary. They were the lowliest of the army of people who labored to make a movie, and seldom appeared dressed in anything but the roughest overalls.

I could not believe that they would do anything of vital importance to a picture, sick or well—and said so.

"Of course not. They just do what Jim tells them to do. He's in charge of everything."

"Who's Jim?"

"Jim Melvino. He's just a cutter, too, but he has a knack with doctoring sick pictures."

"Would he be in charge of me?"

"Oh, sure. And the title writer, the boys, the story and all the film."

"Mr. Corcoran too?"

"You bet. Corcoran's got a sick picture. That gives him a black eye with the company. It's on the shelf."

"On the shelf?"

"Can't be sold. Too bad a picture to be released. A dead loss. Hundreds of thousands of dollars. So even if Jim wanted to change the story, shoot some new scenes, even a whole sequence, Corcoran will let him. Jim gets whatever he wants. You would have an office in the scenario department."

So I moved into Metro and met James Melvino, an ungainly, six-foot-two beanpole of a man, unschooled, untaught, unmannered, who ruled like an absolute monarch.

He spat when he talked, pimples covered his face and dandruff the shoulders of his coat; his clothes, from the torn cardigan down to the stained white sneakers belonged on a scarecrow. But he intruded into the offices of directors and stars with impunity, showing them where they had gone wrong.

No one questioned his orders or decisions. His only difficulty was in conveying subtle nuances to those too dull to understand.

But I understood. I could always sense something—a meaning; and something that had beauty and fragrance,

behind his helpless flounderings. We got on well. He heard
Dick Hyland call me Molly and after that the name was
often on his lips.

"Molly! Where's Molly? Find her and ask her to come
to my office."

So I learned the techniques—title writing, cutting,
and doctoring sick pictures. What I wanted to learn was
continuity writing.

This was different from every other kind of writing, a
definite craft. The original story had to be changed into a
script, a book of stage directions, as definite as the plans
and specifications given to an architect. When a continuity
was finished and approved, copies were sent to department
heads, cameramen, actors, all who worked in the company.

Some writers were particularly good at this and
developed big names. Directors and companies competed
for their services. There were four, and they all happened to
be women, who, it was said, received from four to eight
thousand dollars for each script they wrote. Mostly, they
worked at home, visiting the studio for necessary conferences.

I longed to take my place beside them. My pen name,
I decided, would be my two first names—Mary O'Hara.

The scenario department at Metro was a thin, one-
story building, one whole side of a big quadrangle planted
in the center with grass and a few shade trees. The writers'
offices were small and all alike, but the one at the end, for
Mr. Blakeman, the head of the department, was large, and
suitable for conferences. At the other end was a big room
for half a dozen typists and desks and supplies.

Every studio had a number of continuity writers on
their staff. They sat in those little offices, hammered out
their continuities and received a weekly pay of a good many
hundreds of dollars. But not much prestige. Hack writers,
they seemed to me.

I soon got to know and like the Metro writers. Most of

them were men. Each office had a door opening on a sort of roofed and paved arcade. The doors always stood open. The writers visited back and forth, to talk themselves out of a jam, to get a new viewpoint, or gripe about some unreasonable order.

The moment I saw a continuity—and they were on the shelves in every office—I knew I could write one. I visualized it instantly. I wouldn't have to learn. Any writer could write one, or so I thought, not knowing that everything hung on that power of visualization.

There were also new terms to learn: *fade, lap, pan, dissolve,* and so forth. The rest was just a matter of arranging words in the proper format.

So many of the difficulties that I had anticipated proved so illusory that I set myself a task. I put a book, a classic, on the table before me, opened it to page one and ordered myself to put it into continuity.

I might as well have asked it to read aloud to me. I went to the neighboring office where an experienced "hack" writer was pounding away at his machine and asked him, "Freddie, how do you know where to begin?"

He hardly looked up. "Just tell your story."

I walked back to my office thinking that would be easy. I knew all about stories—I'd been writing them all my life. But before you tell it you have to find it and, in the book, there is a mass of verbiage to hunt through. Seldom does the story, the right story, begin at Chapter One. Many a continuity writer has lost his job because he couldn't find the story.

For me this analysis of the material was familiar work and I did it easily. Having found the story I could apply Freddie's words. I never forgot them.

When next I needed advice, I went farther down the row and asked an older man. "Some of the story is told in action, some in titles. How do you decide which?"

He was thoughtful and I surmised it was a moot point.

"You can tell any amount of plot in a title, but if there is an emotional scene, give it to the actor. That gives him a chance to show what he can do."

I've never forgotten that advice either. There is hardly a script I have written when I have not been helped by it to an important decision.

I was ready to try my wings.

I went all the way down the row and talked to Mr. Blakeman. I told him I was ready to do continuity and asked him to give me a chance. They needed more continuity writers at the studio and I soon got the chance— a writer became ill when his script was half done. Mr. Blakeman handed it to me.

"See what you can do with that. It's a big melodrama. The director's howling for it."

I went to work on it with enthusiasm.

During this time I was beginning to get the feel of the studio. The competition was fierce. Where was the real ability and where the sham? No one knew so everyone was mistrusted. Not a very happy place. Nearly all were far from their homes, lured to Hollywood by impossible hopes.

The overlord of the entire western division of Metro had his offices in a sort of cupola at the very top of the studio complex. He was rarely mentioned by name—we called him simply the "Big Boy." Or perhaps just jerked a thumb upward with a twist of the mouth. Somehow he seemed to know everything that went on.

The studio crawled with snobbishness. Jim Melvino's longing to mingle with the great on an equal footing was inordinate, but their doors remained closed to him. He was embittered and resentful, explaining to me it was because he was a cutter. They ought to give him the title of editor on the credit line when the film showed. They knew he had the brains.

I thought to myself that grooming would serve him better. Get rid of pimples and dandruff. Get a good tailor. I thought I might give him that motherly advice when I knew him better.

There were several miniature theaters where a company could inspect its day's work. Everyone concerned, the stars and directors, were eager to see their work on the screen—the "rushes"—before they went home. But for everyone else it was a routine chore.

One time I attended with Jim, glad to sit among the mighty and see my titles flashed upon the screen just as they would appear before the public.

A director's voice complained, "That close-up of Elsa. She's supposed to show surprise but not terror. Run it again, please. I think she shows terror." It was run again and again. She showed terror.

Elsa Marvel, sitting beside me, said meekly, "I'm sorry." There must be a retake.

"Isn't there a smile on the face of the straightfaced comedian, Henry North?"

Henry's voice out of the dark, "Not a smile, just a hint of wry humor to give it a touch of satire."

Jim decided that one. "No wry humor. Just a poker face."

On one occasion the "Big Boy" had sent down a guest to see the rushes. A secretary brought him in and placed him alone in a row of seats.

When several shots had been run, he said, "But there was a title in one of those shots which was ungrammatical."

Everything stopped.

"I am the title writer," I said. "What is wrong with it?"

I felt on trial. My expertise with words and grammar was at stake. Would I have the courage to speak up if I was right, or admit it if I was wrong? On such things a whole career could depend.

The visitor said, "That word *pondered*. It needs the word *on* after it. The title should read, 'He pondered on the alternatives.'"

It would have been tactful to agree, but I never thought of such a thing. Remembering the many arguments, often about words and sentences, in the Brooklyn house, almost hearing my father's laughing voice saying, "Go to it, Mary," I said, like a schoolmarm, "Pondered is synonymous with weighed. You couldn't say 'He weighed on his alternatives.'"

Trifling episodes of this sort passed around on the studio grapevine with the speed of a telegraph. I encountered smiles and knowing looks and began to feel I had an audience.

I was easily accessible, eager to learn, and flattered when anyone asked my help. They began to come to me from all departments. From the art department, where a talented designer, just a boy, had made two beautiful drawings, the head of a flight of stairs on an upper level and the landing below where it ended.

"I thought I'd just check with you before I take it to the boss," he said, a little shy.

The designs were beautiful but something felt wrong.

"What happens next?" I asked.

"When the boss has approved them, I'll take them to the carpenter shop. They'll build the sets."

I held the drawings, studying them, and finally said, "This is a spiral staircase. By the time it reaches the lower level, wouldn't it face left?"

His face blanched. He took the drawings. One glance showed him the horror he had almost perpetrated. An error like that would have cost him his job. And why not? Such sets are costly.

I liked to do whatever I was asked but sometimes it

was unreasonable, such as when a director with whom I was only slightly acquainted came to my office with his star, Louisa Mont, and a hairdresser who was close to tears. He complained of the elaborate way she had done Miss Mont's hair. The character wasn't a queen, or even anyone of importance—just a schoolgirl. The scene couldn't be photographed until the hair was right.

The hairdresser tried to smile. "I've done it three times."

"And each time it was worse. It's costing the studio thousands of dollars." He suggested perhaps I would be so kind as to do Miss Mont's hair myself.

Very politely I refused, saying that there was no reason Miss Mont should not do her hair herself the way she used to do it when she was a schoolgirl.

A studio had filmed a story with an important episode midway through in which the heroine lost or relinquished her virtue. Filming was completed and the actors dismissed, but the studio had trouble editing it and the film could not be released. That crucial scene left the audience uncertain. Had she or hadn't she? It needed an explanatory narrative title. That would settle it. All the studio writers and writers borrowed from other studios attempted that title. None were right. They seemed ridiculous or coarse or common or censorable.

They borrowed me. I went to the studio, they ran the picture for me, I wrote the title in half an hour. The picture was finished and released.

My hairdresser, upon seeing the picture, said to me, "She went the limit with that guy, didn't she, Miss O'Hara?"

"What made you think that?" I asked out of the soapsuds.

"Well, that title, where it said, 'She had given her happiness into his keeping.'"

Hollywood agreed that when it came to titles, I was

the Queen Bee. Also I had the "common touch." I was
getting a name and earning good money.

My script was finished at last. Before giving it to Mr.
Blakeman, I wanted Jim's opinion. He read it and came to
my office the next afternoon.

He was quiet and absorbed in thought as he sat down
in one of the big armchairs, leaned back and stretched out
his long legs that reached half across the room. He put his
elbows on the arms of the chair and carefully fitted the tips
of his long bony fingers together.

There was a silence. I sat without speaking, not
wanting to miss a word, sure he must be surprised,
bursting with hope and confidence.

At last he said solemnly, studying his fingers, "It's
really awfully bad."

The strange, almost absentminded way in which he
said it suggested he was really puzzled by such a degree of
awfulness.

The nervous distress that went through me in succes-
sive waves was physical. I sat there, agonizing. But I
wanted to know more.

At last he said in the same strange ruminating way,
"If that came to me to doctor, I don't know what I could do
with it."

That was what he was ruminating about—such a
script, made into film, and given to him to doctor.

"Because you've made them do all the wrong things
and written it so well that if I take it apart, I'd just have
hash."

At last I found enough voice to speak. "If they didn't
do all those wrong things I made them do, what could they
do that would be right?"

"Just act naturally."

I never forgot that.

Added to the shame I felt was the fear that I might

have gone down so in Jim's estimation, that he wouldn't want to bother with me any more. I need not have worried. His thoughts were not on me and what I had done but on that awful piece of script and how he could possibly take it apart and doctor it.

He was still as crazy about my writing as ever. It was like an addiction. He carried loose pages of my writing in his pockets. Talked about it to everyone. He said he had never read such writing. I was able to say and say easily things he had been trying to make people say for years.

I did many more scripts. I was accepted now as a Metro continuity writer. I never turned one in without checking first with Jim. Directors began to ask to have me do their scripts. My lucky streak held.

I was sick of living in rented houses. I bought a plot of land where a new development was opening up on North Rossmore Street, near the Wilshire Country Club. The golf links would adjoin my back garden so, even when houses crowded around, from my imagined back upstairs window, it would look as if empty country stretched for miles westward to where the setting sun fell into the sea.

I planned the grounds. For privacy, a six-foot-high brick wall all around and French poplars inside the wall. A lily pool in the center of the garden. I planned the lovely house too. It was just a dream house, but the lot was bought and paid for.

Every so often a moving picture is made which electrifies the world. One such, *The Four Horsemen of the Apocalypse*, had recently come out. The director was a young Irishman named Rex Ingram, and Metro had got him and his beautiful leading lady, Juli Temple, who was also his wife, under contract. New York was looking for a big story worthy of his talent. Meanwhile he would do whatever program pictures he was told to do.

Here was someone new and exciting to watch. He made several small pictures and we were astonished at his casting. He used the most unlikely actors, who then looked marvelous on the screen. To the anguish of the company, if he did not like a story they gave him, he spent his days out on the back lot playing football with his staff.

One day Mr. Blakeman telephoned me to say he was sending his secretary to my office. She would take me to Mr. Ingram, who wanted to meet me. We went and I was introduced to the great director.

He looked too young to be so famous. There was not a mark of experience on him. It was a refined face, completely masking the cruelty and wickedness which emerged in his pictures. He was very quiet, as if always slightly abstracted. He could have been twenty-five or forty-five. He was mysterious, like every true artist.

We chatted for a while. I wondered what was coming. Then I noticed a pile of scripts about eight inches high lying on his table. As he saw me looking at it he laid his hand flat on the top of it.

"These are the best continuities I have ever read," he said and I leaned over and saw that they were all mine.

That strange quiver went through my nerves that we call a thrill. He was going to ask me to do a continuity for him and I was eager to assent.

He explained that the place of continuity writer in his unit was at present empty and I leaped to the conclusion that he was going to offer me the post and was not too happy about it. The writer who wrote for Rex Ingram could write for no one else. But he had more to say and I saw there were conditions attached.

She must also be his reader—read everything on the market, help him choose stories, make synopses of everything. She must be at his side when he directed. She would supervise the cutting. Their private conferences could be held while they lunched or drove to locations. She would be, I saw, his alter ego. She would have no independent life whatsoever.

It was not at all what I wanted. What I wanted was to be out there with the few famous continuity writers who worked free-lance, who worked where they wanted, at home or at the studio.

But they had more than merit and skill, they had big names. As yet, I did not. But if I became Rex Ingram's staff writer, even for a short time, I would achieve one.

I asked him for a few days in which to think it over. Then I accepted his offer.

21

Big Blond Swede

The inner workings of picture-making are so complicated a matter, involving so many people, that for me it meant the exclusion of everything else, though matters of far more moment were going on in the world—the war. World War I.

It was as if a giant cauldron had boiled up and spilled over. America was drawn in and joined its allies. Our young men went overseas; our young women drove French ambulances. Those who had to stay home and care for children or old people worked endlessly for the Red Cross, making bandages and dressings, knitting sweaters and mufflers.

Mrs. McGill, a very delicate-looking little woman, lived with me and helped me bring up my children. She was a Scot, that warrior race which strikes terror into the hearts of its opponents by marching into battle with swinging kilts and whining bagpipes. In the Great War, the Germans called them "The Ladies from Hell."

The new songs were all war songs, such as "Keep the Home Fires Burning." O'Hara sang that beautifully. Kay preferred a more martial air. Mrs. McGill described his performance, ". . . marching down the middle of the street with a big empty whiskey bottle under each arm and shouting at the top of his lungs, 'Over there! Over there! And we won't come back till it's over, over there!' Oh, Mrs. Parrot, he was grand! Just grand!"

Everyone was affected by the war.

When it ended at last and people resumed normal duties, many lives were so altered they never could take the same shape again.

It would be honest to say that this was true of me, though I did not know it until considerable time had passed. For it had brought to this country a big blond Swede whose name was Helge Sture-Vasa.

He was the son of a diplomat who believed that the time of internationalism had come. He sent Helge, for several years, to an American prep school, the Virginia Military Academy, called VMI. The family had a summer place at Eagleshields Bay in northern Sweden, a landed estate in Belgium, the home of exiles and internationalists, and a large country place in Africa.

When the war broke out Helge was in Berlin, studying picture-making techniques at the UFA Studios. Warned by German friends that if he didn't get out of the country fast he would be interned for the duration, he got over the border into Belgium and joined the First Queen's Cavalry, of which his father was the colonel.

Later he transferred to the American Remount Service. He became an American citizen and at the end of the war planned to resume his studies of moving pictures, not now at the UFA Studios but at Metro, in Los Angeles.

There were many war refugees trying to get work in the moving-picture colony, most as actors. The lists of the casting directors were full to overflowing. Others sought work in the technical department, as it was called. This was where the sets were built to match the scenes described in the script. A man had to be expert with hammer and saw, able to read blueprints and improvise when necessary.

Helge got this sort of job.

The refugees who could do nothing but act could get work only occasionally. Some were very aristocratic and came from different parts of war-torn Europe. Besides distinguished manners and bearing, nearly all had titles (or so they said). Among them were two princes, one pretender to a throne, several dukes and a good many counts and barons. We called them the Hollywood Dukes.

They were immensely popular and would have been on the top rung of the social ladder except for the fact that they never had any money. Only when a scene was to be shot showing a coronation, or a glittering ballroom, would the casting directors call them up. Then they would don the brilliant uniforms, dance, bow, philander, or dismiss a lackey, all with a certain foreign grace, difficult for our American actors to emulate.

During those years at Metro it seemed to me I was simply besieged by men.

From time immemorial the human female aged fifteen to fifty has been pursued and usually caught by the human male, provided she is pretty, has a good figure, charm, magnetism, sex appeal or any other form of come-hither. The exceptions are if she is an upper-class French girl and never for as long as a half minute out from under her mother's eye; or if she is safely held within a convent wall; or if there are simply no men about.

But where I was working in Hollywood, there were plenty of men about. Everyone knew that Willis Goldbeck, Ingram's publicity man, was hot on my trail; that I spent hours closeted alone with Jim; that I had been seen in the arms—I should say rather in the grip—of a big cameraman, for he had caught me from behind in a narrow corridor; and that when the leading man of the next production simply could not be found, look for Mrs. Parrot.

In such a milieu an impregnable defense had to be conjured up—an attitude that was positively forbidding. It became second nature to me. I wore it like a shield even when I did not need it. With Rex Ingram, for instance.

Rex was in love with his wife, Juli Temple. It was moving and disarming to see the way his face changed the moment he laid eyes on her. It made one feel that all the good things that have been said about men and women are eternally true.

The type of beauty she had was the beauty of innocence: children, flowers, morning dew. He worshiped that, too.

But this was not the real Juli Temple at all. That was someone Ingram himself had created for her movie roles and the studio built up until she seemed this ethereal creature, floating several inches above the earth, capable perhaps of a faint smile but never a frank, hearty laugh. This was her "persona," presented to the public.

Her real name was Ani Stengal and she was the youngest child of a respectable German family living in Milwaukee and working in the brewery there. Ani, because she was so pretty, was sent by her family to Hollywood. What Ingram loved in her was that illusive beauty he himself had created. I wondered if that would hold him forever. I think it did.

At any rate, I soon knew that I need not be on the defensive with him. Yet I was, and only gradually did I find out that there were other ways a man could victimize a woman than by pursuing her. He often asked me to read to him and explain a passage that was risqué, even obscene. Soon I knew he was doing it on purpose, always making sure to have an audience watching and listening.

Once, having drawn attention to me, he said, "Just look at her. She always looks so clean." Coming closer he looked me up and down. There were about fifteen people watching. Then he reached out a muddy shoe and drew it across my instep.

As a piece of stage business guaranteed to make the audience hate the man who did it, this could not be improved on, and I used it in a story.

Ingram was shooting a war story and needed an actor for the part of Bersonin, the villain. He must be young, six feet or over and able to ride like a Uhlan officer. The casting director chose several from his list, then went looking for Helge, whom he had seen on horseback one day, and asked him how he would like an acting job? Helge needed money and said if he could get it he'd take it.

By the time I saw him he certainly looked a thoroughgoing villain in the worst German-officer style. Ingram had made a long sabre scar across his cheek. He was in the uniform, riding boots, helmet, sabre, and all.

I think it was what he had done to the boots that got him the part. New riding boots are painful to wear and as shapeless as if they were made out of wood. It is said that Napoleon Bonaparte had one of his aides wear his new riding boots for six months before he himself would put them on. But Helge knew a way to break them in and had taken the trouble to do it.

First having (painfully) got them on, he had greased them thoroughly with neat's-foot oil, then stood ankle-deep in water till they were soaked through and soft, and walked in them till they were dry. So treated they were shaped to his leg and foot and comfortable too.

Ingram noticed those boots, and remarked that no other of the aspirants for the part had taken the trouble to make his boots look as if they had really ever been worn.

One day I went onto the set and saw Helge there among the other actors and said to him, "So you are our Bersonin?"

At first I was amused and intrigued by a man so

different from all others. At last I was simply bowled over by him.

Because we were both in Rex Ingram's company, we were thrown together every weekday, but seldom alone. Crowded into cars being carried to location or busy on the set, we had arrived at the companionability of strangers who work together. However, sometimes on weekends he had asked me to go out with him, dance, swim, or ride horseback. The riding I loved. He was a wonderful horseman and could do things with horses I did not know could be done. So I went riding with him and began to feel that he was at my beck and call.

But a good many others were too.

One evening we worked very late and Mr. Ingram asked Helge to see me home. At my front door I turned and reached out my hand for good night.

Our foreign contingent never shook hands, they kissed hands. It was as automatic and casual a gesture as shooing away a fly, but when Helge took my hand, bent his head and pressed his lips to it he gave it meaning. It was like a vow, a dedication which he meant me to understand.

When he left and I had shut the door I stood in my living room with my heart pounding. I was shaken all through. This was real. Something I would have to deal with. Something that could alter the shape of my life forever.

When, a good deal later, he made his proposal it was no surprise to me. The words were humble, almost fearful: "Would you marry me?"

One cannot help feeling that there is something fateful about an event as important as a marriage. Yet when we come to record it and find that it came about by the merest chance, even by a series of chances, almost impossible chances, we are struck with wonder. And then we remember that legend always portrays Fate as a weaver, who sits, smiling as she threads many colored strands through her loom thus creating patterns one could never imagine.

During the last year I worked with Ingram we had the good luck to make a big historic film, *Scaramouche*. It was such a success and gave Metro such *éclat* that they decided to send the Ingram company to the French Riviera to make three pictures at lower costs.

Everyone would go. Mr. Cheney, Ingram's business manager, came to my office to talk to me about transporting my ménage, the two children and their nurse, and did I want a maid, or could I wait till we got over there?

When I told him they would have to go without us, that I could not possibly leave the country, he could hardly believe me. My relationship with Helge was too important.

For many months now, stone masons, carpenters, plasterers had been busy at 201 North Rossmore. Soon after the Ingrams left for Europe, the house was finished and furnished. I wrote my father, and told him I was going to be married to an American citizen who had been in Belgium, in charge of American Remount there during the war, and who had afterwards come here to work in the movies. Elma was with Papa at that time and I wrote her too.

Papa answered with a special delivery letter full of demands: "Do not marry him without first finding out all about him. Who is he? You must have letters from his family. You must see his passport. Don't be in a hurry."

When Elma got mine she told me she went running into his study. "Papa! They're married already! Look! She's sent a picture of him!"

She handed the newspaper clipping I had included to my father—the photograph of a straight-standing, direct-eyed young officer with a row of medals on his chest.

A detailed inspection of the picture at last brought a favorable verdict. Papa liked his face. "But who is he?"

22

The Happy Marriage

This, my second marriage, was a happy marriage. It taught me that nature's ways are not always cruel. Men are different. Marriages are different.

Helge had made friends with my children beforehand. They not only liked him but were excited about him. Somehow he belonged to us.

But not all my friends approved. Fanny insisted that he was a fake. He had just pulled the wool over my eyes. And when I laughed at this and described the intimate details about the family life he had told me, she said, "Of course. But he was the footman. The groom. The valet. You'll see."

Others said that I was marrying the same kind of man I had married the first time.

Nothing could have been further from the truth. Tall, handsome and commanding he was. So much was the same. But Helge did not stand apart from people, or laugh at them, or intimidate them. He had an understanding and compassion that drew people to him. He went out to them. He communicated with them. With me. And this made all the difference. It made of him not only a husband to whom I surrendered, but a friend and companion, walking at my side, my hand in his. If I had worries I could tell them to him.

There were no worries now, but a vast fund of information that was a delight to give each other. I told him of the long step I had taken away from my sheltered upbringing in Brooklyn to where I stood now, and he told me of the much more terrible things he had gone through in order to meet me here.

Once I asked him how far back he could remember. To the age of three? Four? He recalled a time when he was a year and a half, and his parents had given him a toy bicycle and it had fallen to the floor and he was trying to pick it up with one hand and balance himself against the wall with the other. The wall, except where the tapestries hung, was cold to his little hand. Then a laughing girl snatched him up from behind (was that his mother?). His parents were always doing that and he did not like it and struggled to be put down so he could get the bicycle. This must have been in Eagleshield's Bay, Sweden, because their house there was stone.

His next memory was of their place in Africa when Helge, standing at the gate of the grounds, heard the frightening sound of a runaway horse. He jumped out of the way. It was his mother on the horse. As Helge told me of this he put his hand to the side of his head and said, his eyes widening in memory, "Those perfect curls all disarranged—the hat dragged down—"

His father galloped after her.

"And what happened?"

"They turned a corner and I couldn't see. I don't remember anymore. But of course he got her. Father never failed."

He talked a great deal about his father, who, evidently, had expected his son to follow him in the career of international diplomacy. He took Helge with him when he was called upon to settle the Fashoda Incident, a dispute between France and Britain, which was holding half a dozen nations on the brink of war over control of the upper Nile. Helge, fourteen years old, had sat on a stool in the corner of the room and watched and listened while his father, with curt, commanding arguments, brought the disputants to their senses and so prevented the war.

Then he casually related something that seemed very strange to me. "He took my sweetheart away from me once. It was when I was at Uppsala. I introduced him to her. I was so proud of him. But after that she hardly looked at me, she had eyes for no one but him. He said, 'Forgive me for this, my boy. There will be so many more for you. But not for me.'"

These were just vignettes and that is the way he told them, as if he had put a pair of binoculars to his eyes and glimpsed now this, now that fragment from his past.

There was one memory which brought so charming a scene into my mind's eye that it made me smile—a small boy sitting at breakfast in a baronial hall with his grandfather, who was a Scottish laird, while outside on the garden path, a highlander in kilts paraded up and down, playing his bagpipes.

It was like being given a few pieces of a giant picture puzzle and out of these, trying to reconstruct the whole. I doubted if Helge himself saw the whole. But of course that could be said of anyone, even when life had not been broken into pieces by a world war.

Some of his most fragmentary—and most terrible—recollections referred to events after the war when he and his two American friends had engineered an expedition to explore the headwaters of the Amazon River.

I never could understand this expedition. It was done on a grand scale with forty native bearers to carry their supplies and impedimenta. The finance might have been provided by one of Helge's friends, who was the son of a multimillionaire. There seemed to have been something laudable about it. It was to provide scientific information.

Yellow fever struck the camp. The native bearers absconded leaving Helge and his two friends, one already in a coma, the other raging with fever, and the river, which was the only hope for help, fifteen miles away. Of the whole episode, getting those two men to the river was the only part Helge had a clear recollection of, for he carried them. One at a time. Five miles with one, then five miles back for the other. Helge could tell me little about it for the fever was already in him, held at bay, as it were, until he got his friends to safety.

That was Helge. He got to the river with two dead men.

When at last the fever left him and he had regained consciousness, he was in the house of Dr. Emilio Hernandez of Durango, Mexico. But all he could say about it was how unlike himself he felt, he was so weak, unable to do anything. It felt strange to be in a wheelchair, with someone behind pushing it down the long station platform. The story was incomplete and mysterious and I asked many questions to which he could answer only by shaking his head.

I did not doubt anything he had told me, the very strangeness of those little vignettes vouched for their truth—the toy bicycle, the disarranged curls, the bagpipe breakfast. But I wanted to probe all the empty spaces in his past life and I could not. The marvel was that he was here, safe and sound, on the garden patio talking to me, the picture of health and better looking than a man has a right to be. I should be content with that.

Well, I was. Content and thankful.

Presently we began to talk about the children. He wanted them to call him "Father." Also he wanted to take complete charge of them, so relieving me of that burden.

"There has to be discipline and training," he said. "And if I do it, then they can escape from me, the drillmaster, to you, the little sweetheart."

I knew that in Europe it was considered that American children were badly brought up. This could not be true of mine, they had nice manners and obeyed me. But it was true that it required endless haggling.

I wondered what Helge could do that I had not done. I soon discovered. They had to make their own beds and often I saw the beds ripped open after they once had been made, and had to be made all over again. And O'Hara's hour of piano practice before breakfast could not be five minutes short of that, no, not one minute short.

Kay had got into the habit of leaning against anything he happened to be near. Now, his feet would be whipped out from under him and he would be sent sprawling to the stern reprimand, "Haven't you got any pride?"

To offset this Helge would make a special after-school snack for Kay when he came home at three in the afternoon. At that hour the kitchen was empty. To fry an egg on both sides it had to be flipped. Helge would flip it, Kay watched, amazed at the smooth way it would rise above the little skillet, turn in the air, then sink back into the hot butter without a splash. Then some chunks of onion would be cut up and all put between two pieces of rye bread. I would hear the voices in the kitchen as they talked.

One day Kay presented himself before me, very erect, thumping his chest. "I'm getting to have some pride," he declared.

It did not take him long to decide that when he grew up he wanted to be a man "just like Father, because he can do anything."

I had often thought of West Point for Kay instead of a civilian college, if there was only some way to get him in. I had once attended a hop at the Point and had never forgotten the cadets. So straight, clean, and groomed; and already in their eyes the look of men under command and in honor bound.

Soldiering was in the tradition of our family. There had been a General O'Hara in the Revolutionary War and in the war just past a Colonel Brereton had been often in the headlines. Periodically the Military Academy issued statements extolling the training as preliminary to civilian life. The graduates would be ready for war if and when it came. Helge thoroughly approved and was sure Kay could get in.

I had worried about how O'Hara was going to get along with Helge—a big, nearly grown girl with a stepfather who was also a disciplinarian. But when I sounded her out, she looked at me in surprise and said, "Why, Father's the best thing I've got."

She had fallen for him.

Well, so had I! And I never knew a child who did not.

So there was no dissension between either of my children and myself on the score of the stepfather I had given them. On the contrary, they went along with me. They backed me up. We were all glad we'd got him.

There were other things in him I loved, hardly to have been expected, and I listed them proudly—for instance, his love of beauty of every kind. He would hurry to find me so that I would not miss the rapidly changing sunset clouds at the back of the house. We would stand silent, hand in hand, watching while the rose and gold merged, faded, thinned and drifted off, disclosing a sea of emerald. There, in the green sky a golden star.

Or music. So often, when I was at the piano, just improvising, he would come in, sit down and listen. Would sometimes ask me to play one part over and when I asked which part, he said, "That lovely, free, wandering melody."

Not to be left out of the list of his virtues was his wisdom about drinking. It was an important part of the education of young people because nothing was more certain than their meeting the problem sooner or later. Americans did not know how to drink; they simply got drunk, which was a disgrace. The children must be taught how to drink the way his father had taught him—eat something, take a swallow of wine, put the glass down, eat some more. And, in a given time, never more than a specified amount of alcohol.

I never saw him drunk. He took up his glass and drank with pleasure when others did. But in an era when a great deal of hard liquor was served at every party and there were always a few men who got drunk, Helge never did. He was never even noticeably affected. He would be the one who took the drunken ones home. Or got some sot out of the living room into the garden just in time.

We bought a Cadillac touring car. I say "we" because it really was "we." He helped me in everything: the household errands, fetching and carrying of the children. When there was an evening party, he took them to it and went again at midnight or so when it ended and brought them back.

He ruled over this small domain wisely and well. It seemed to me unfair that it was so exclusively *my* domain. My children and my servants, my house and my earnings. He was so well qualified to have a much larger kingdom and to be its natural lord. Of course I shared everything with him.

We drove to Santa Cruz one summer. I wanted Helge to see the mountains that rose so swiftly from the sea beaches to steep peaks, the fine roads that curved and climbed, wooded on both sides but opening here and there.

One such place, a balustraded stretch, gave a glimpse into a deep gorge below through which ran a torrent of water. The water leaped the rocks and boulders, throwing spray into the air and forming waterfalls and green pools for rainbow trout to play in. From it rose a sound like no other sound on earth—ceaseless and hypnotic. The burbling of a mountain stream.

We drove higher and higher. There were trees and streams all around us. Here and there, by a stream almost shut in by trees, were small cabins the style of a Swiss chalet. Helge spotted many good sites for such buildings. Though he no longer went to the studio, he had not forgotten the sets he had built in the technical department. Besides, he had a natural talent for building and a love of it.

That drive to Santa Cruz cost us a good deal. Before we left we had bought a cabin site down a bank from the road where there was a natural flat terrace beside a stream. There he would build the weekend place for us to run away to. Farther away, on an upland stretch, we bought fifty acres filled with madrone trees which, he was sure, he could cut up, build cottages on and sell.

At different times we drove to all the beautiful seaside places up and down the California coast in the Cadillac: San Diego, La Jolla, Ventura, Pismo, Santa Barbara. It was on one of those long rides that Helge began to talk about the future. It surprised me. His past had been enough to overwhelm me. And the present, full and happy and brimming over with things to do. That there should be room left for a future that would not be just a continuation of the present was almost a shock.

He told me he had made plans to go into the sheep-raising business in Wyoming after the war. The man who would be his partner was Bill Carlson, who lived in Wyoming and knew all about it. Carlson had been his veterinarian when he had been assigned to the American Remount Service during the war. Fortunes were to be made in sheep-raising, Carlson had told him. "Firemouths" they used to call the sheep, because they nibbled so close. There had been war between the cattle men and the sheep men. But that was over now. The sheep ate what the cattle and horses left.

Helge said it was practically a sure thing if you could get the right sort of a ranch, and it was big money—really big money. Hundreds of thousands of dollars.

As Helge told me about this I was struck with his expression as he described the rigors of the climate, the snow and ice, the wide-open spaces, so much uninhabited country and his face lit with eagerness.

"How would you like that?" he demanded, taking it for granted that I would pull up stakes and go with him wherever he wanted to go.

Well, and so I would. Why not? I could write anywhere. Give up the screen writing and concentrate on short stories. And it seemed to me just the sort of thing Helge needed now. Uprooted from his home, stripped of everything he had, he needed a new beginning. This would be it.

Not that I thought it was ever really and truly going to happen. But he could plan and dream about it. That might be enough.

On the ride home on that same day, he added, as it were, a postscript. It was to be taken for granted that sooner or later he must return to Belgium and see if anything could be recovered of his family's possessions. The Germans would have destroyed and taken everything they could, of course, but land cannot be destroyed and the title to that would be held for us.

"By whom?"

"The crown."

I asked him what he meant. He explained that he meant Brabant, king of the Belgians. Brabant, I gathered, was a familiar form of address which the king's equals, for instance a Vasa, would use in addressing him.

This reminded me of something else he had once said.

He was admiring a dress I was wearing and said, smiling, that it reminded him of a dress worn by Kaiser Wilhelm's daughter. He had noticed it one day when he was lunching with the family at Potsdam.

It was clear what Helge expected me to understand. He was a Vasa, and a Vasa, if not exactly a king, was of royal blood and hobnobbed with kings.

Fact? Fantasy? Or a mixture of the two stirred up by a man who was a born raconteur, and who, besides, may have been slightly deranged—shell-shocked, they called it in those days. Few men who had gone through the war were not.

Well, what did it matter—how much was true, how much false? There were the Hollywood Dukes. No one cared if they were real or fake, provided they played their parts well and could be used. But they took themselves seriously.

What we Americans knew about royalty was the excitement and romance of the many stories that were written about them, such as *In the Palace of the King*. Or *The Prisoner of Zenda*. We all knew about the heir to the French throne who was stolen at birth—the dauphin of France— and speculated about it to this day. And there were the two little princes in the Tower of London.

Helge said he was followed every day of his life when he was a little boy by a Swiss guard, lest he be stolen by those who wanted to see a Vasa of the old (the true) line on the throne of Sweden. It was something not only believable but a wise precaution.

The evidence accumulated. Generations back, a Hohenzollern had married a Vasa princess. Ever since, now and then there appeared a Hohenzollern with a Vasa face. The kaiser was one of these.

One day when Helge had been working at the UFA Studios in Berlin and they were out on location, Helge was carrying the camera. Crowds were watching them. In the crowd a German officer kept his eyes fixed on Helge and finally approached him and asked if he might know his name. When Helge gave his name, the man's hand snapped up to the salute and he clicked his heels.

When a man has such adventures to relate he is certain to be disbelieved by many and called a teller of tall tales at the least. But that he could have been a complete fake as Fanny insisted, masquerading, trying to deceive me, was, on the face of it, impossible, because he was a gentleman. The imprint of truth was on so many of the little things he told me. No, a liar and deceiver could not invent such things.

And yet, when I finally reached bottom, there was a lie somewhere. There was something he was hiding from me and did not want me to know. Perhaps he would tell me in time. Perhaps not. What matter. I would not ask him about it or worry myself. I knew he loved me. I loved him. We were happy. Let him keep his secret!

But the truth is not so safely mocked. There are stories within stories in an autobiography.

Many years later, when we were living at Santa Barbara, something had reminded me of Papa's warnings about Helge's background. I heard myself say to Helge quite unexpectedly, "Do you remember when Papa asked for your references and we laughed it off? I think I should not have. Would you get some now? Perhaps a letter from your friends, that prince something-or-other whom you often mention. Or your international passport from The Hague."

His reaction astounded me. He made a stiff bow and said formally, "I shall try to do what you ask in spite of the passing of two wars."

He looked around the room with a slight sardonic smile. "Well, it's been very pleasant living here, knowing you."

He made me another bow and went about the room

gathering up his things—pipe and tobacco pouch, his gloves. He was heading for the door.

I gasped, "Are you going away?"

He paused long enough to look all around the room again, saying, "I am a complete stranger here."

Without a glance at me, he took his coat from where it hung on the back of the door, went out, got into the car and drove away.

I don't know how I got through that day.

That evening, Helge returned.

I had dressed carefully. I was in a yellow gabardine coat and skirt. I was standing. He crossed the room quickly to me, his face white as I had never seen it before. He took me in his arms and said, "Oh, Mary, I've been so wrong about everything." I burst into tears. The moment of truth at last.

At that moment Lena opened the swinging door to the kitchen to come in and set the table for dinner. We each sat down in a corner of the sofa, both of us drugged with the strain and tension, and now sudden relief. We fell asleep while she set the table.

The moment of truth never occurred again.

Again the lie had submerged.

23

Are You Available?

At last I took my place beside those few favored mortals as a free-lance continuity writer *with a name*.

The gossip was that Mary O'Hara had got her big name by refusing one picture after another. In a way it was true, because I believed that the elements of excitement had to be in the story before it was made into a picture, whereas the producers thought all depended on getting famous stars and directors and spending limitless amounts of money.

My opinions were in the minority in those days, so, to make good on them, I had to be very careful in choosing only good stories to work on.

The call would come in the morning when I was having my breakfast in bed, sitting straight up against my pillows, the tray flat on my knees. The telephone stood on a table within reach of my hand.

At the first tinkle of the telephone, my nerves tightened.

"This is Paramount Pictures speaking. Is this Miss Mary O'Hara?"

"Yes."

"Are you available, Miss O'Hara?"

To accept an assignment was, for me, not only the labor and difficulty of writing—eight weeks of creative writing—but also the certainty of heading into trouble. A finished picture left many a corpse on the battlefield. This was not only sometimes, it was always.

This being so, and realizing as I look back on those brawls that I am smiling, there must be humor in them. I thought at one time of collecting them into a batch of brawls—short stories—and calling it *Are You Available?* It was one of those ideas for a book which never came to birth, but a few will fit in here showing another side of my work.

Most of the difficulties are between the director and the writer. The writer has to break the original story down into separate scenes, each one numbered; the director has to make the actors perform as the writer has described. The head of the story department watches what they do, approving or disapproving, and himself is watched over and checked by the producer.

When I was engaged by Warner Brothers to do a script to be directed by Liebendorf, I was warned in advance that he simply demolished his writers, that his producer, Henry Compton, had vowed he would make him toe the line. There must have been something about the story I liked or I wouldn't have taken the job. Scare stories about Liebendorf I didn't worry about. They can't eat you alive.

I had a good contract with eight weeks to do the script. The time element, I found, was why producers hated Liebendorf so. He never got through when he ought and that meant the producers had to give enormous weekly checks to everyone working on the show—perhaps twenty people.

I went to the studio, met my director, was happy to find he was quite an attractive young-middle-aged man, and sounded him out about letting me work at home, with frequent visits to the studio? No, he liked to work more closely with his writer, and he showed me my office, right next to his, with an open door between.

This went against the grain with me, but I worked out all the preliminary analysis and blocking out without interference from him. He was perhaps too busy entertaining himself with visits from his friends who flocked to see him. There wasn't a day that he didn't spend hours talking to visitors in his office. Sometimes he would call me into his office and we'd run over together what I had done. Nothing but approval.

But weeks were passing and I began to be seriously worried about my contract and my deadline. Henry Compton called me frequently, almost every day, asking how I was getting along with Liebendorf, to which I answered, "Fine."

"Would the script be done in eight weeks?"

I said I felt sure it would.

I never, until the last ten days, had the least doubt about getting that man, one way or the other, to stop fiddling around and do his job. We settled down to work one day. My typewriter had been moved into his office and we were going full speed ahead when a visitor knocked at the door, opened it and was warmly welcomed by Liebendorf, who then turned to me and said that would be all today.

"No, Mr. Liebendorf, we've got to finish this sequence. I'm sure your friend will excuse us."

My skill in remembering the very words has deserted me now. He was the maddest man I've ever seen—being told in his own office what he could do and not do. He roared and yelled at me. Metaphorically speaking, he tore me limb from limb. I began to weep. Soon I was in a terrible crying fit. At last I began to shout at him too.

The studio got strangely quiet. No typewriters going,

no footsteps running up and down the halls. I was telling him at the top of my lungs, between my sobs, what a brute he was.

The deadly quiet persisted when it was all over, the guest had gone, and my sobs were just sobbing breaths.

At last Mr. Liebendorf said, "You beat my wife when it comes to epithets." (His wife was the famous vamp Sheila Dawn.)

"Also the hankies," he said, pointing to the row of tear-soaked handkerchiefs I had arranged along the window sill.

After a silence he said quietly and meditatively, "But I still don't understand what made you so awfully angry?"

Breaths were still sobbing breaths, but I managed to tell him. "Because of the way you—personally—treated me."

At that he gave a long "Oh—oh—oh" of comprehension and then said, "Well, Miss O'Hara, I'm not a gentleman, and you mustn't expect it of me."

The telephone was ringing in my office. I went in to answer it.

It was Mr. Compton, even more anxious than usual. "How are you getting along, Miss O'Hara?"

And I answered with the usual, "Fine."

"Are you going to get it done on time?"

"I'm sure we will, Mr. Compton."

And we did.

Reports of such combats spread rapidly. This one did no harm to my reputation or prospects. I was commended on two counts. One: I had got Mr. Liebendorf ready to go into production on time. Two: I had put on a "magnificent" dramatic scene of my own.

Another result was that Mr. Liebendorf and I became good friends. He wanted me to write for him again but this honor I declined, making convincing excuses. Better let sleeping dogs lie.

Another combat worth being recorded was when Universal Pictures asked if I would do the script for a story they had just bought, Dorothy Fisher's *The Home-Maker*, so exactly suited for a moving picture that every studio must have wanted it.

It was puzzling that Universal had got it. I decided that someone in the eastern office, keenly sensitive to dramatic values, must have spotted it and acted quickly. In this I was right.

For the story to have been sent west to be made was routine, but what difficulties it created! How could a studio like Universal make a story like that—delicate, sensitive, with a part for a child that nearly made you weep just to read it. Universal was a very rough place and made nothing but rough-and-tumble pictures. Their staff of directors, writers, supervisors, editors, and executives was constantly changing, one lot being fired and a new lot taken on.

The man who was to direct the picture, King Baggot, wore a chronic expression compounded of hostility, resentment, and frustration. Not a pleasant man to work with.

Dorothy Fisher's lovely story had been thrown to the wolves. I wondered if there was anything I could do to save it.

Then I learned that Doris Frome had quite recently been acquired by Universal as story supervisor, and began to see light. It must have been she who asked for Mary O'Hara for the script. She was nobody's fool—a nice woman who knew dramatic values, as well as how to behave and treat other people. Between us we might get Mrs. Fisher's story on the screen without its being chewed to pieces.

Then came the familiar tightening of my nerves which told me I was going to war. So, tentatively, I went out to Universal and was passed from one rude, illiterate employee to another till I began to wonder if anyone out there could read or write. Probably not.

I had not entirely decided whether to take the job until I met and talked to Dorothy Frome. I liked and trusted her. Best of all, we both liked the story and hoped it could be saved from mutilation.

As we talked, several times there were distant sounds of doors slamming, angry voices, and Miss Frome explained with a slight grimace, "Joe Rafferty, head of this unit, has just been replaced. A lot of underlings go out with him. It was he who hired me."

"But you're still here."

"Perhaps just on probation."

"Who's taking over?"

"Arthur Varney."

That was bad news. He was a czar and liked to throw his weight around.

Then I went to the legal department and settled business matters. I had long since taken the stand that I would never sign one of their long, regular form contracts. I wrote my own, two short paragraphs on one sheet of writing paper: one-third of the fee on signing, one-third on delivery of the complete outline, and one-third on the delivery of the finished continuity. It put them in my power and they hated it, but they had to take it or leave it. After all, they knew I would play fair. I knew they wouldn't.

I spent the rest of the day with my new director, King Baggot.

I wrote the script at Universal's offices. It was an easy one to do, the characters so well drawn, their actions so natural, so inevitable, it was just a matter of technique to translate the flowing tale to a series of scenes for a camera to shoot.

In the many hours that I spent on the job with King Baggot I never saw one smile, not even one kindly look or one nod of approval. Unless it was when I wrote one entire episode in pantomime.

Pantomime is regarded highly in picture-making. To write a scene so that the mere silent gestures of the actors can tell all that must be told requires great skill. The danger is always that the sense of the story will not come over clearly.

I took the chance.

In a general revision I lost my nerve and took it out. Mr. Baggot's lowering brows drew lower and knotted in a frown. He was ready with a reprimand. "You had a fine scene done all in pantomime. Now you've taken it out. You are overwriting."

"Oh, did you like the pantomime? You didn't say so. I'll put it back."

To maintain cheerfulness of demeanor while I fed my budding ideas into that scowl was almost too much for me. But I kept the peace and at last the script was finished. I sent it in to Miss Frome and gave myself over to golf.

I heard nothing from her for a week, which did not surprise me as a good many people would be reading it.

Then she sent for me. The script lay between us on her desk. She put her hand on it.

"Rejected in toto by Mr. Varney."

We looked at each other in silence for a long time, then I asked her how she herself felt about it.

"If Universal wants to film the Fisher story," she said, "they couldn't get a better script than this."

"But Universal doesn't want to do it," I replied. "Someone in New York started the project. I wish I knew his name."

"Why?"

"We could send the script to him. Get his opinion."

"Go over Varney's head? My dear, I couldn't. It would mean my job."

"But I could."

I shipped the script airmail, addressed just to "Story Department."

Both Varney and Frome received the telegram, "O'Hara script excellent. Hurry production *Home-Maker*."

Of course Mr. Varney found out who was responsible for getting that order from New York countermanding his rejection of the script. I wondered if he would retaliate. But obviously there was a real war going on, for in a matter of days Varney was gone and Jacob Stilling sat in his office.

These changes at the top made no difference in King Baggot. He plugged along, angry and sour and scowling. One thing in favor of the production was that it was making good time.

When it was about two-thirds done it ran into some trouble. Universal prized noise, liveliness, belly-shaking comedy gags above all else. Walter Ruby, an actor with an inexhaustible talent for devising gimmicks and stage business, was much in demand at Universal. Mrs. Fisher's story had no such moments but there was a child star, Stevie, to be played by four-year-old Jackie Cooper, and where there are children, there is always a place for ridiculous nonsense. Universal staff writers, when they reached the scene with the child, wrote in *Hokum ad lib*. Then Walter Ruby would come with his fat smile and belly and jazz the scene up.

I was working at home on another script when Doris Frome telephoned me, telling me that Universal was "sending for Walter Ruby."

"For what scene?"

"Stevie's big scene."

"Not the transformation scene?"

"Yes. Where he gives the drink of water to his grandfather."

It may be thought that Mrs. Fisher was taking a big chance when she injected into a story a scene showing a change of heart in a four-year-old and expected it to be caught by a camera. But those of us who have had children have seen many such changes and can also remember the amazing frequency with which the small fry demand drinks of water.

Mrs. Fisher's description of the child's countenance, besieged small animal at bay, was a masterpiece of word-painting. But when he offered the glass of water to his grandfather, he was crying. I had to put the book down and walk around for a minute or two before going on.

Doris Frome continued, "I've called a conference about it. Tomorrow afternoon. It would be a big help if you could be there."

Everyone was there. Walter Ruby beamed at me, "You missed a chance there, Miss O'Hara."

"What do you think I should have done with the scene, Mr. Ruby?"

"Why, when you get a little kid on the screen, you can do anything! Rough 'em up. Get him standing on his head. There were a dozen laughs in that scene once you get it going."

Several voices agreed loudly with Ruby, and others stopped to listen. I held the book firmly under my arm. We were now the center of attention. It was a chance for everyone to have his say and I welcomed it.

Doris Frome and I took our seats. Jacob Stilling came in and sat down at a desk, turned toward us and leaned his head on his hand. I did not know whether he was a friend or an enemy. I could tell nothing from his expressionless and tired face. As he did not call for order, the scene escalated and everyone who thought they knew how the picture should be made announced it fortissimo.

The book was my defense. Time and again, I lifted it to quell the noise and say, "Just a minute, please," and then read a sentence or a paragraph of Mrs. Fisher refuting the crippling, moronic nonsense they offered.

Jacob Stilling never moved, but I saw that after every argument his eyes turned to me to see what Mrs. Fisher had written. He was saving himself the trouble of making any more decisions about it. He was going to do it by the book.

When it begins to be bruited about in Hollywood that such-and-such a studio has a hit, there is great excitement. For in spite of all the king's men and all the king's horses and their concerted efforts, a hit show is a rarity.

The first suspicions that this was a hit came when it was in the editing department, and cutters and editors were talking about it.

"Wait till you see this!"

"Not *Universal!*"

At last the reels of film were sent to New York.

There was silence for a week before the newspapers burst out with praise—Universal Pictures had made a beautiful picture, a classic, an example to the other producers.

Last of all Mrs. Dorothy Fisher's enthusiasm and gratitude, "God bless those men in Hollywood."

24

Orange Blossoms

When Kent had told me, long ago, that the legal profession would be for him just a means to an end, the end being a career in politics, my thought went immediately to our games of chess. Traditionally, chess symbolized the maneuverings of a monarch against his opponents. Kent, then, had achieved his ambition, for he was now the political boss of Los Angeles.

It was the vice-president of my bank, a good friend of ours, who first told me of it. Not a single business deal of any size or importance could be put through without Kent's consent.

"He sits up there in his big regal office overlooking the city and rules it like a king."

The cartoonist of the *Times* pictured a large bird, obviously a parrot, smoking a cigar, giving orders to a small cringing man who looked like the mayor.

One reporter got an interview with him and put the question, "Why do you take all this trouble if you get nothing out of it?"

And Kent replied, "I get a kick out of it." An answer

so like Kent—it gave me a good laugh. It was widely quoted.

I wondered what had become of Porter, Morgan, and Parrot? There was no sign of them.

Los Angeles was festive that winter. Everyone was in the market and making money. It was the long, famous bull market that led up to the great 1929 crash and depression. Kent was in that market and I heard of his giving a hundred-dollar tip at the club. That, too, was like him. Perhaps it went with being a boss.

I now had to ask Kent's help about a very serious matter—getting an appointment for Kay to enter West Point. I hoped that was something a boss could do.

Kay was fifteen, so handsome a boy that I had written and sold a short story about him, with the title "The Too Beautiful Boy." It was time his college was settled upon.

Sometimes a divorced pair become enemies and hurt and defame each other constantly. Kent and I had never done this. It was as though we had made a pact with each other to be friends. Once before, soon after the divorce, in those first days when I was so desperately hard up, I had telephoned him to say that though the court had awarded me something for the children's support, he had never paid a penny. And he had answered, "You can't get blood out of a turnip." So he had been hard up too.

He had come a long way.

I approached with confidence the downtown building where he had his office. It was a large office, handsomely furnished and appointed, with a view from the windows.

Kent was very well dressed, and as good-looking as ever. We chatted for a few minutes, and then I told him why I had come. Everyone knew he was a power in the state now. Did he have enough influence to get an appointment to West Point for Kay?

There was a telephone at the end of the long table at which he was sitting. He tilted his head toward it.

"Nothing easier. All I'll have to do is pick up that telephone and ask the senator. Kay will get the appointment."

It was good news for me. I left his office feeling that something very important had been accomplished.

But the matter turned out differently. The senator either could not or for some reason was unwilling to get Kay the appointment. This was not only a bitter disappointment, it was demoralizing. I was crushed.

It was Helge, Kay's stepfather, who suggested that Kay could still enter West Point if he was willing to take a much tougher road, which, in the end, is what he did. Kay spent a year in the army as an enlisted man. This made him eligible to take the competitive examination for an appointment.

He took it and passed it and in 1931 received orders to report to West Point. He was in.

When O'Hara was ten I sent her to boarding school, the Ramona Convent, much the best school in the neighborhood. Her unusual voice and musical talent gave her prestige there immediately. When she wanted to join the Catholic Church, I knew that meant she believed and she cared. I gave my willing consent.

A visiting monseigneur, before taking his departure, said, "And I would like to meet the little prima donna who sang the solo at benediction."

O'Hara was brought, kneeled before him, and he gave her his blessing, making the sign of the cross over her head. She prayed for everything she wanted, reciting Hail Marys rapidly under her breath.

One day she tore loose the tongue of her low shoe and carried it around the corner to the shoemaker. He was busy but it was a little job—his wife would do that for her. She was a deep-bosomed Italian peasant woman with dark hair parted in the middle and drawn back on either side. She looked like a Renaissance painting. She put the shoe on the low work bench before her and O'Hara leaned close, watching. The first needle broke. The woman took another.

O'Hara began, "Hail Mary full of grace, blessed art thou among woman." The Italian woman's deep voice joined in. Woman and child finished it together, "Blessed is the fruit of thy womb, Jesus."

The needle did not break this time.

O'Hara liked to genuflect deeply in church and never forgot to cross herself before eating. Nor to tell me that I should be doing the same. She grew tall and straight with the long tapering fingers of her father.

At the piano she could easily strike two notes over the octave. This gave the bass of all her improvisations and original arrangements a strange quality—the supporting tenth instead of the usual eighth. When she sat at the grand piano in our Rossmore house, the sounds wafted out the open window and people would stand in the street, listening.

These little incidents struck me then and have remained in my memory. There were others. The high dive she made off the end of the pier down at Santa Monica— that ecstatic scream of joy at the peak of the swan dive as she leaped up as high as she could, with head and arms thrown back. It seemed to say, "See how beautiful I am and how I can ride the wind!" Then the slow turning of her body leaning on the wind, as it turned, wheeled and then plummeted, straight as an arrow, down into the green depths of the Pacific.

I remember one more incident. When she first heard Beethoven's *Fifth Symphony*—the opening five notes of which have been interpreted as Fate knocking on the door—she burst into tears and could not stop crying, as if she felt the call had been meant for her.

Coming events, they say, cast their shadows before them. If such shadowing takes the form of a premonition, one discards it almost angrily. Later, if the premonition comes to pass, one says, "I knew it all the time." My premonition about O'Hara came to me when I bought the satin for her wedding dress when she was only fifteen. There would be years to wait, but it was too beautiful a piece of satin to miss when it was there on sale at Robinson's, thick, creamy charmeuse, as soft as chiffon and the end of the bolt. If you wait to buy white satin for a wedding dress when you need it, you are likely to come home with satin that is stiff and rigid.

But as I laid the lovely stuff away in the bottom drawer of my chiffonier and put blue tissue paper over it, I felt a shadow fall on my spirit. Would the dress be unlucky?

Shortly afterwards O'Hara fell ill. She complained of a headache and nausea—it did not seem very serious. I had often been as sick myself. But it got no better. I called a doctor and he diagnosed it as meningitis. She was very ill indeed. The doctor said that she would not get over it. There would be a little improvement, and then she would become worse again. Another doctor was called in for consultation.

O'Hara was sick a long time, and grew very thin. Once while she was at the hospital for tests that were to be given early the next morning, I came to her bedside to say good night. I leaned over to kiss her. She clutched and held me.

"Mummy, will I ever be well again? Really well?"

"Of course, darling. Young people get over their sicknesses."

"Promise, Mummy?"

"*Why, O'Hara!*"

"Promise," she insisted. So I promised.

But it was not to be. A number of years later she died in her sleep.

The doctors finally diagnosed it as Hodgkin's disease, but I knew it was the blue mole.

O'Hara wore her wedding dress after all, but she had grown so thin that I had to lay the folds of the creamy satin one over the other, and hold them in with a narrow band of gold at the waist, then draw them down her long legs. Her feet were beautiful and I left them bare. Her masses of titian hair I brushed up and back. It filled the space around her head and curled into her shoulders. I filled her hands with orange blossoms. Her face was serene and inscrutable—the little star.

At the cemetery, her own father, Kent Parrot, was present but he stood far off, not near where I stood, beside the open grave, the encircling ring of loose earth ready to be shoveled in after the coffin. His face was shadowed and greenish.

As is the custom, they opened the lid so that she could be looked upon one last time and I, almost unbelieving, saw the same face I had seen at her birth—serene and inscrutable, and quite separate from me.

She had never looked lovelier nor more at peace.

I questioned Kent with a glance. If he came and saw, would it not be a comfort to him to remember her thus, that little mite, that small flannel bundle whom he had held so proudly in the crook of his left arm when he brought her from the nursery to my bedroom in the Gramercy Park Lying-in Hospital? He shook his head violently.

I signaled the attendant to close the lid, and watched while they lowered the casket into the grave and the first shovelful of earth fell upon it.

For O'Hara, the leaping and singing and praying on this earth was ended.

25

Wyoming

I have now reached the Wyoming chapter of my life.

When I am asked where my real home is, I reply, the East Coast, the West Coast, and the Rocky Mountain Divide—for Wyoming is right up there on the summit of the divide, that almost impassable wall of mountains, running like a jagged backbone from north to south dividing this country into two parts. High and ever higher one lifts one's eyes to those peaks and ranges which mingle their everlasting snows with the clouds.

When Helge and I reached Wyoming we found that we had not merely gone from one state of the Union to another, but had stepped off of one planet onto a sphere that orbited at a different tempo, under different skies, under different orders. It was a wholly different world. It was transcendently beautiful. Vast. Empty. Glowing with heavenly colors.

Hills and mountains were behind us now. The sky, a deep cobalt, was like an inverted bowl cupped over us coming down to the horizon, which was low and very far away, seeming to be on a level with us. Between us and that distant horizon stretched the grass, a flat carpet, bright emerald green; cloud shadows lay upon it here and there, very dark, purple or midnight blue, constantly changing their mysterious shapes. Way off, almost invisible, was a cluster of antelopes, just tiny dots. They looked like figurines on a lady's table.

We were short-cutting across old Wyoming dirt roads and hardly altered our fifty-five-mile-an-hour pace. But the scene did not change. It was like being in a trance— traveling strenuously, but getting nowhere. It made us silent and spellbound.

So this was Wyoming, I thought, a secret hidden world unknown to the rest of the country, serene and calm, with a slow heart beat.

I had been ready to escape from Hollywood. Escape is the right word because one sickened of Hollywood, the stresses and strains, ambitions, rivalries, jealousies, betrayals. A man who had worked in the movies for years told me that, while out driving one day, he passed within a half mile of Metro, and such a wave of nausea engulfed him that he had to stop his car, get out and vomit.

But that was not all. As time went on I was coming to know myself, and beginning to realize that what had always been considered shyness in me was actually almost claustrophobia. I didn't want to be shut in, couldn't endure crowds. In fact, I wanted a great deal of solitude—freedom from the pressures of people always around me, pressing upon me, making demands.

I created with my imagination a vista which gave me much comfort. A view of great mountains, with a jagged skyline at night. There was no moon, and at the lowest part of the picture there was bottomless darkness. I called it the *Wilds* and it comforted me the way a line of Whitman's

verse comforted: "Night. Sleep. Death. And the stars."
The movies made me sick for the *Wilds*.

I thought about Wyoming and the sheep-raising now
and then. Helge mentioned it quite often. I wondered if it
was something that was really going to happen.

One day he wrote Carlson, who lived in Cheyenne,
and later made a date to drive up there to see him. He left
our Rossmore house in Los Angeles one morning in the big
Cadillac touring car and came back a few days later in a
Studebaker, explaining how much better it was for the
rough roads of Wyoming. He had seen Carlson, who was as
keen as ever to carry out their sheep-raising plan. They had
driven around, looking at various ranches.

From that time on Helge constantly talked about
Wyoming; the different breeds of sheep: black-faced,
Rambouillet, Corriedale; the advantages and disadvantages
of each, as he recounted to me all that he had gathered from
Carlson.

It would be cold in Wyoming, he told me, real winter
weather. Snow, ice, blizzards. This delighted me. I was
tired of southern California's patios and swimming pools,
and all the year-round flowers. This would be like my
childhood in Brooklyn Heights.

I began to feel as I have often felt on a high dive,
looking down, just ready for the plunge—butterflies
rushing all through me. It was really going to happen.

I was ready for Wyoming. I did not believe it would
make the fortune Carlson assured us it would. It might
perhaps even lose money, but I was going to make no
objections. Let the men decide and take charge. If not a
fortune, something else good would come out of it. It was
in the line of my destiny. I had a hunch about it.

It was almost as if I had intuited the fact that in
Wyoming I would meet and get acquainted with those wild
horses which roam our western plains. And, unless that had
happened, I never could have written "My Friend Flicka."

Helge made a good many more visits to Cheyenne. The Studebaker made nothing of the thousand-mile trip between the two cities, though it included a crossing of the Mohave Desert, where a good many motorists got into trouble with a hot engine.

The plan Helge and Carlson had made was simple. Helge would buy the ranch and the sheep, in fact whatever needed to be bought. (This money would come out of our shared bank account, into which I poured all my earnings.) Carlson would supervise, make important decisions, guide and provide the earnings, and they would share all profits, fifty-fifty.

Those profits would all depend on how many six-month-old lambs they could raise and sell a year. They were worth fifty-five or sixty dollars a lamb. A band of three thousand ewes would need one herder and a ranch of one thousand acres. So they counted their chickens before they were hatched. The final figures were impressive and accounted for the popularity of sheep-raising.

Helge already had his eye on a ranch thirty miles outside of Cheyenne on the Lincoln Highway, ideal for sheep. Three thousand acres. His face was aglow.

The part of the ranch which was tucked into the foothills of the Rocky Mountains consisted of the home buildings: the log ranch house, a bunkhouse for the hired men, a number of sheds and outbuildings, and a big barn, set deep down into the earth for winter warmth. The barn had room in it for all the animals that might need to be sheltered there. The interior was like a cathedral, three stories high, divided into pens and stalls and separate compartments. It had a peaked roof, made of the straight slender poles from Pole Mountain which the state supplied free to anyone who wanted to cut and transport them.

"I would call it the Remount Ranch," he said, "because all this started when I was in charge of American Remount in Belgium."

If anyone had told them that there was an adversary to their project—not a sheep disease like anthrax, or the maraudings of coyotes, or the never-ending fights between beef growers and the "firemouths," but a distant, invisible, impersonal entity called a "market," which could reduce one of their sixty-dollar lambs to the value of an order of lamb chops which you would buy in a hotel restaurant and which would include for your sixty cents two small lamb chops and a sprig of parsley—they would simply have said that such things can't happen.

But that is exactly what did happen.

The long bull market which preceded the depressions of the thirties, and which had made my former husband rich, had thrown the whole country into a state I can only call drunkenness. People rushed to buy and become rich overnight.

Nothing quite like that boom had ever been seen in this country before. Hard times were gone forever. You really didn't have to worry about money anymore. Just buy into the market.

The man who owned the ranch which Helge named Remount eventually sold it to us at his own price. We sold all our California holdings and moved to Wyoming. We were followed by a Mayfair van with our furniture and my grand piano.

26

The Ranch

When people speak of the market crash of 1929 and the Great Depression that followed, they often speak of the depression in the plural—depressions—for it was really a series of them. The first thunderclap came when one heard the shocking things about millionaires committing suicide by jumping out of their office windows. Then there was a pause and people took hope and thought it was just temporary and things would recover again. Then came another, deeper slide downward and the banks began to fail. The government had not yet passed the law which guaranteed the deposits. Mortgages and loans were called. More and deeper plunges downward occurred until everyone who had anything lost it, or, to be exact, ninety percent of it. The Denny Estate was bankrupt—whole blocks of houses stood empty. People had no money to rent them. Middle-aged, dignified-looking men stood on street corners trying to sell apples for a nickel each.

What Helge and I had left was the ranch. When the sheep had been sold, given away, or turned loose to fend for themselves, when Carlson had gone, for there would never be any profits, when the sheepherders were gone, and the hired men, what we had left was a couple of work teams, great hulking horses with heavy shocks of hair over their hooves, some milch cows and a bull and the usual small fry of cats and dogs, chickens and ducks, a dozen or so horses, mostly half-broken broncos with a few old faithfuls who could be ridden, and any wild horses which had come in from open country on to the unfenced portions of our grazing land.

That was our home for eleven years.

The rest of the country gradually shook itself loose from its ruins, staggered to its feet and slowly tried for a new beginning. We did the same, trying and failing at delivering milk in Cheyenne, catching some wild mares, breeding them to a government stud and raising the colts for polo, and finally starting a summer camp for boys, which downgraded us to the level of a dude ranch, but was the only thing at which we had ever broken even.

Keeping a ranch or farm in good all-around shape entails grueling labor which never ends. This is a well-known fact. Add to that a soldier's high standards of cleanliness and order. Helge was constantly making improvements. The dump with a broken plough and the twist of old pipes, barely covered over, must be dug up, buried deep, grassed over. Walls of sheds and outbuildings, not one of them perpendicular, must be straightened. Even the main house, which, because the ground under it had not been properly leveled and graded, ran a little downhill, would have to be practically rebuilt. A narrow terrace in front, running the whole length of the house, Helge decided, would help. For aesthetic purposes, he decided to build a wall about two feet high to hold up the terrace, and place a border of flowers around the base, using the blue iris that grew so plentifully in the meadows. A Dutch door, the kind which is built in two sections, upper and lower, could be added, painted the same cobalt blue as the Wyoming sky. Half of the terrace, he decided, would be shaded by a pergola—from which a hammock could be hung underneath. And in another part of the terrace, an iron pot, an old Dutch oven which he had dug up from the trash heap—filled with ivy and myrtle, and a few bright zinnias.

Birds gathered around that pergola. Especially when, inside the house, with the upper half of the Dutch door open, I was playing the piano. Neighbors could not understand it. Were we trying to make a summer resort of the ranch?

No, just a home.

Upstairs, on the second floor Helge wanted to build a fireplace in my big bedroom. His room, next to mine, was only large enough to hold his bed, the small table beside it and a chair.

My bedroom was also my writing room and had my two typewriters in it, my L. C. Smith on a big solid table and a little Corona portable an arm's length away on a small table with wheels, for often I worked at two stories at a time, finishing up one on the L.C. Smith and jotting down notes for the next on the Corona. In fact, that is the way I got the notes that turned into "My Friend Flicka."

I never gave up the effort to find a subject which would simply enthrall the reader and consequently be an immense success. At that time the name of an important German author was much in the news, with criticisms and excerpts of his latest work, a sort of treatise on marriage and its value in developing character due to the great amount of strain it subjects the married couple to.

Since I found his ideas interesting and had some ideas of my own on the subject, I had decided to write a story about him. Just let some of his ideas come home to roost. I put it on the L. C. Smith.

What a character! And a most complicated story. I

had to visualize him—how else could I describe him? And
he turned out to have a beard.

It was hard going. I was laboring at it. Depending on
whether or not a story had already matured in my mind
with several scenes ready to pour out, my writing went
quickly or slowly. This one was going very slowly. Why
should I have to labor so?

At last I stopped and rested, analyzing my difficulties.
The subject was not a familiar one to me. I could not
chatter about it, almost without thinking, the way I
chattered—for instance—about my animals. When I told
little stories about them, I noticed that people stopped
what they were doing and listened.

Everybody is interested in the hundreds, the thousands of wild horses that are in the American West. Many
stories have been written about them, and whenever a new
one is written, you can't get it for the longest time at the
library. Suppose I wrote one—how easy it would be—about
that little filly, for instance, the one that got caught in the
barbed wire.

First I could tell something about the horses—
descendants of the wonderful Arabian horses, brought to
this continent by the Spanish; how the horses went wild,
drifting up to California and other western states, pro-
liferating, surviving by their speed, indomitable spirit,
intelligence, and endurance. There are many magnificent
specimens among these horses—when one is caught and
tamed, as sometimes happens, he becomes a superlative
mount for a cowboy.

Suppose a little boy caught and tamed one? I reached
for the Corona and drew it toward me. I did not give up on
Herr Doctor, that was going to be an important story, but
meanwhile I would make some notes on this other.

I worked the rest of that day and half of the next.
Inside of twenty-four hours the notes and a few scenes of a
short story entitled "My Friend Flicka" were written.

*   *   *

Helge felt a good deal of compunction—almost a sense of guilt—at having brought me to such a wild and lonely country. For him it was not so bad because our ranch was not more than fifty miles from Fort Francis Warren, an army post with all that went with it. An old soldier himself, Helge was quite at home there and made a good many friends with the wives and families of the officers. They had a big ballroom for Saturday night hops. Or a crowd of them would go in to the Plains Hotel in Cheyenne, the one big high-class hotel.

Aside from this there were many little cafés—"joints"—where Helge liked to sit alone with a cup of coffee before him when he shed his ranch responsibilities for a few hours.

None of those diversions were open to me except an occasional dance at the post. I went to the Cheyenne library and was friends with the librarian. Also with the pastor of the Episcopalian church and his wife. No one else. I was often—indeed most of the time—desperately lonely for social companionship with my own sort. Helge knew it and grieved about it.

I had often thought of getting us out of the hole we were in by my stories. I worked very hard at it, stories like those of de Maupassant or Hawthorne. As they say, stories will not be accepted unless they are slanted to one magazine. I slanted them toward the women's magazines with which I was most familiar. They were beautifully copied on the L. C. Smith, well packaged, stamped, and addressed. Every one came back with a rejection slip.

One day in the fall after the first light snow had fallen—giving notice that the summer was ended and the long winter closing in—Helge brought news from Fort Warren that Captain Daws and his family were going to Los Angeles in a few days. How would I like to go along? The captain would be delighted to take me. There was plenty of room in the car. They were going on down to La Jolla. It would give me a break and if I could connect with someone at the studios, I might sell something. I could come back on the bus.

We did no traveling these days except by bus. We seldom could afford even that.

I was glad to go. I had a nice visit with my old pals and talked with Blakeman, who was still story editor at Metro, but it was the same old business. They didn't buy originals for the screen.

I showed him "My Friend Flicka," which I thought particularly good screen material. He sat and read it through while I was in his office and handed it back to me with a smile.

"A good little story," he said, "and as you say, tip-top material for the screen. But to get it there, you would have to turn it into a full length novel, take it to New York, get it published by a good publisher, then it would have to make the best-seller list. After that your New York agent would offer it to us for fifty or a hundred thousand dollars, we would buy it and film it."

We both laughed.

I said, "When I was writing here I used the Forbes and Sykes Agency. Would I have to go to a different agent in New York?"

"You sure would. And a good one. Without that those New York vultures would pick your bones clean. I mean your brains."

He could not know how eager I was to have my brains picked. "Who are the vultures?"

"The publishers, of course, the lot of them. And their families, even their dear old mothers. And their assistants and editors and readers and scouts."

"But, Joe, if the publishers are going to buy my story, first they have to want it. What's wrong with that?"

"They don't buy your story, they buy certain rights to it."

"Rights?"

"There are screen rights, foreign rights, condensation rights, recording rights, braille rights. Lots of others. Your story remains your literary property. It is your capital. The continuing sale of various rights and anthologies is like the interest your invested capital draws. But right here is where many an author has been ruined. He's so anxious to have his story bought and published he'll sign the first contract they shove at him."

"How can his agent prevent that without queering the sale?"

"Just by crossing out a few little words in the regular contract they'll expect you to sign."

"What words?"

"*And all rights.*"

A telephone call put an end to our talk and I walked slowly away from Joe's office and out of the building.

Riding back to the ranch on the bus gave me plenty of time to think over all that Joe had told me. Taking the story to New York seemed the key to the whole thing. I remembered something else that pointed to New York. It was an article about marketing short stories and it said that editors did not themselves read stories submitted to them unless they came from certain well-established agencies. If only I knew who those agents were. Of course they were in New York.

When I got home, Helge and I talked it all over and he found out how much it cost to go by bus to New York. But we didn't have the money.

During those years when our ranch had been a dude ranch and we had a summer camp for boys, a New York family, the Farleys, had sent their three boys to us, then came themselves to visit us. Elise Farley and I became warm friends and she told me that if ever I wanted to come to New York without having to pay traveling expenses, just to let her know and I could go on one of their cargo ships which went up and down the California coast. Their shipping line went through the Panama Canal and on to New York. So now I wrote Elise, hardly daring to hope that anything so fortunate could happen. But it did.

I took that trip on one of their ships and had some memorable experiences and met a memorable man, Captain Daniels. There were no other passengers and I took my meals with the ship's officers, the two mates, the boatswain, and the captain.

Captain Daniels was a little man and looked like a Frenchman, not at all the type to be in charge of such a voyage. If he had been placed beside me at a dinner party anywhere in the world, I would have found him a pleasant partner, interested in art, particularly music, in people, in world events.

I am not a particularly good sailor. On the first rough day, soon after we had started luncheon, I felt squeamish and excused myself and started to leave the table. But Captain Daniels stopped me, telling me I must eat, it was better so. Go on as long as I could.

The Farleys, having given me this free ride around the continent, extended their hospitality further by giving me a party when I arrived in New York and introducing me to a lot of people.

Unfortunately Ed Farley and I were not at all compatible. He was one of those men who liked to jeer at people and make them uncomfortable. He bombarded me with questions about my trip as if to entertain his friends by poking fun at me whenever he could. How did I like the boat? The meals? The weather? Captain Daniels?

I did not tell him of that last calm evening on board when the little captain and I stood by the rail on the upper deck looking at a heavenly sight—a very thin, crescent moon with a star almost, though not quite, within its embrace. We looked and could not take our eyes away, and at length he said, "What makes it so beautiful?"

I did not answer.

At last he said, "I think it is the star."

I agreed. "Yes. It is the star."

What I did mention was something I thought must have been reported to him already—that dreadful thing, the man who was swept overboard.

"You know about that, Ed? The sailor that got washed overboard in that storm?"

This created such a hubub that it was apparent that no one knew anything about it at all. There were screams, shocked exclamations and Ed's shout, "Oh, don't listen to her! She's just making it up."

I finally made myself heard. "Yes, it's true—a wave washed him overboard; but the next wave washed him on again and this time he caught hold of something and held on."

"It's getting better," Ed shouted. "She's a real storyteller."

There was another outburst of laughing.

Elise carried the talk tactfully away from the ship and back to the ranch, but for the moment I was still clinging to the deckhouse drenched with spray, horrified at the sight of the sailor who a moment ago had been battening down the hatch on the lower deck and was now in the ocean riding a mountainous sea. I could see his legs and arms thrashing about. The deep roll had put the ship half under water. Was the sailor floating over the deck or over nothing but ocean?

My question was answered by the most violent shuddering of the ship. I had made many ocean voyages but have never felt such a thing before. The captain up on the bridge had seen what I had seen and reversed the engines.

For years, Ed Farley liked to recount this tale,

ridiculing me. One wave washed a man overboard, the next wave washed him back on.

Memory often distorts facts and sometimes I asked myself, had I really seen that, my eyes blinded with sea water? But there were the facts. No sailor had been drowned on that voyage, and the captain had reversed the ship's engines.

I had gone back to New York only once since Dr. Parks had baptized O'Hara in Calvary Church and that was when I had wanted to tell Papa I was going to divorce Kent.

I was not out of touch with them, because we all corresponded, but I felt only half a person without Helge. I missed him terribly.

Elma was the first of my family I expected to see. Reese was in London, Bess at Lake George, and Papa and Matrigna at their lovely house in North East Harbor.

My astounding sister had been doing medical missionary work in Shanghai. She had learned the Chinese language so she could preach and teach in it, and had superintended the clinic at the Episcopalian mission at Shanghai. And, when the day's work of making rounds, preaching and instructing was done, in the small hours of the night she would wrap coats around her legs in her cold little room so that she could write stories about her life in China. The manuscript she completed was entitled *My Chinese Days*, and was sent to the United States to Little, Brown and Company, who accepted it and published it immediately.

She had taken a classmate, Dr. Hetty Wismer, to China with her and brought her back to Johns Hopkins when Hetty developed a tubercular knee. Hetty had recovered and got a job as a bacteriologist in a New York laboratory. The two girls took a Greenwich Village apartment with a Chinese houseboy to care for it. Elma was now college physician at Barnard, which is the sister college of Columbia.

Elma, besides her apartment in Greenwich Village among the artists and writers, had a small country place and cottage for weekend sojourns at Westport, and for the long summer holiday a bigger place in the Berkshires—a house, barn, hillside and stream in Tyringham Valley, Massachusetts.

Before leaving the ranch, when I was certain that I was coming to New York, I wrote Elma about my trip and received in return one of her funny little letters, like bulletins. Elma informed me that there was to be an eight-week course on the short story given at Barnard that summer by a famous teacher. She would be leaving for Tyringham the day after college closed and Hetty would be gone as well. I could live in her apartment. Her Chinese houseboy would come in to wash, clean, and cook. I could go up to Barnard every day in the subway.

"I pity you New York in summer. You can fry eggs on the flagstones and if you step on the asphalt it will pull your shoes off. Your classmates will all be college kids but don't be embarrassed. You've never looked more than twenty. Reese says eighteen. The professor's name is Whit Burnett."

27

Columbia University

I wonder which of the forces that play upon human beings is the one that keeps some young, ages others. Is it mental or physical? When I was three or four I watched my father take his daily setting up exercises. He rewarded my interest by showing me how to do them myself, and to this day I have continued.

Some religions consider it of importance to maintain one's youth. I knew a Christian Scientist who said every day, "Fresh, fresh, fresh. Pretty, pretty, pretty. Young, young, young," as a sort of verbal cosmetic. And there is a story in the *Upanishads* about a woman taking a walk in the forest with her children, grandchildren, and great-grandchildren and it said she looked about sixteen.

When I sat in Mr. Burnett's classroom and looked around at all the youngsters, I hoped that I was not kidding myself when I thought that I measured up well with them. Perhaps I was one of those people who are able to stand aloof from the march of years.

There were a couple of very fat girls. I was slender and of medium height. Most of the compliments I had received in my life were for my legs.

When I was middle-aged, a therapist came to see if anything more could be done about my spinal curvature and remarked, incidentally, "You have beautiful legs. But you know that."

My son Kent had always said, "We'll never have to worry about money. If we come on hard times, Mother can model for legs and support us all."

There was not one gray hair in my dark brown mop. But I was fifty-three years old, and I was embarrassed to be sitting with those kids.

I would like to describe Mr. Burnett, but it is difficult. He was of ordinary height, ordinary bulk, ordinary feature. There is only one thing I remember when I think of him. He had an absolute poker face. He never smiled. Perhaps I can give a clue to his nature by reporting daily battles he had with a big electric bell in the hall outside of his room which began to yammer about mid-lesson and kept it up for at least twenty seconds. As the sound began, Mr. Burnett would—without saying anything or cracking a smile—rise from his desk, go out into the hall, and tear that bell from the wall. A repairman would repair it and reattach it that afternoon. The next day the same thing would happen again.

Whit Burnett was the editor of a monthly magazine of short stories which was called simply *Story*. It was famous, though it never paid more than twenty-five dollars for a story, because it had broken with the boy-meets-girl-and-they-lived-happily-ever-after type of story; in general, with old familiar patterns drenched with sweetness and light.

Every year Whit Burnett put out an anthology called *The Best Short Stories of the Year*. He had an imprint of his own, though he was not actually a publisher, nor a writer to any extent.

For the first few weeks he lectured mostly on style, with interesting examples by Walter Pater and Robert Louis Stevenson. He detested the former and extolled the latter.

The students scribbled furiously in their notebooks.

Then he announced that he would like to see some samples of stories written by students. He pushed a wire basket to the corner of his desk. If any student had a complete short story ready for the publisher, he stated, just place it in the basket and when he got around to it he would read it to the class and discuss it.

A few manuscripts were placed in the basket, among them "My Friend Flicka." One afternoon Mr. Burnett took them home with him; he brought them back the next day.

He told the class to stop scribbling notes. He was going to read three stories aloud to them and wanted them to be ready to pass judgment on them.

I could not help the slight trembling that shook me. An important—almost climactic—moment in my life had arrived. I told myself he would save the best of the three to the last.

He announced the first, "Minnie Takes a Bath."

A little giggle ran over the class. What could any writer do with such a subject? The author didn't do much and the entire class rejected it, saying there was simply no story to it.

But Mr. Burnett carried it around for them to look at, drawing attention to the perfect format, the excellent typing, the loving care she had lavished on it. His final opinion was that she would probably make it as a writer someday.

He read next a story which was titled "The Gin Bottle." The short lecture he delivered afterwards made up in vituperative power for its briefness. He pointed out that many young people go to college, major in creative writing without knowledge, talent, or even an average quota of brains. Perhaps it seemed to them easy work—just get a lot of words on paper and the money and the kudos would come. "I assure you, you'd succeed better at garbage collecting."

My own cheeks burned with shame for the poor young man. I thought I had spotted him.

Mr. Burnett laid "The Gin Bottle" down and picked up the last manuscript—"My Friend Flicka."

He was an excellent reader. Each story had been read in a way to get the most out of it. When he finished my last words, "gentle as a kitten," he laid the manuscript on his desk and looked at the class. Everyone stared back at him but no one spoke. He waited, looking from one face to another, and at last said impatiently, "Well?"

A voice said, "The best of all."

Someone else said, "Much the best."

He suddenly got up from his chair, holding the manuscript in his hand and roared at me, "Did the filly die?"

The whole class turned to look at me, having not known until this moment who the author was.

"Yes, she died," I answered, "but I always thought that if I had gone down there to her, and stood by her to the end, I could have saved her."

He stood silent, thinking. The class too was silent until he spoke. "And that's your story."

A babble of talk broke out. They clustered around me. Someone asked him, "But, Mr. Burnett, can she sell it? Will any magazine accept it?"

He walked to me and I received back my little story. Then he returned to his desk. He was thoughtful. "Any one of a dozen magazines that prints short stories will buy it. I may even buy it myself for *Story*. I would have to consult with my coeditors first."

The class was over and the students stood up. Several looked at me. A number of them crowded around.

"Would you sell it to *Story*, Miss O'Hara?" one asked in a low voice. "And get only twenty-five dollars for it?"

Another said, "But you'd be famous then. Forever. And you could sell other stories."

Mr. Burnett and most of the students left but I sat talking to the little group, finding out much about the way short stories were sold. They asked me who my agent was and when I told them I had none, they told me I'd never get ahead without one.

"Why don't you get Sidney Lambert? She lectures here at Columbia on the marketing of manuscripts and she's an agent herself."

This was a very welcome door opening for me. I had been thinking, miserably, how awful to have to write Helge that after all my travel and efforts, I had sold one short story for twenty-five dollars. And even that was not sure yet.

I went home in the stifling subway, drenched to my skin with sweat and excitement, got into a cool shower, then slipped on a negligee while Chung, Elma's Chinese houseboy, prepared a cold supper for me. At last I sat down to write Helge.

I reread his last letter. It made me feel that our days at the ranch were numbered. It was all right in summer with the boys' camp and so many people visiting, but the winters were long and hard and, since there was no way to make it pay, useless. What did I think? Wouldn't I prefer the East? Where my people were? Or the West? California again?

I wrote him a long letter, then sealed it, to mail it in the morning, and looked in the telephone book for Miss Sidney Lambert. I was surprised to find her address was right here in Greenwich Village. I called the number.

Someone answered and told me that Miss Lambert could be reached at her country place and gave the number. At last I had Miss Lambert on the phone.

She answered in a deep guarded voice. She made no responses as I introduced myself at considerable length, until I said that Whit Burnett had said he might buy my little story for *Story*. Then she came to life. An animated discussion ensued of all that had been said, also of any other stories I had brought with me.

Before I hung up I had an engagement to meet her at her house, not a block from Elma's, the next evening.

Miss Sidney Lambert was short and chunky and wore rather flamboyant clothes. She had gray hair about four inches long which curled youthfully all over her head. Her face was pink and pretty. Perhaps it was her voice, enunciating everything with utter finality, that made her seem so grim, but I was charmed by her strength and assurance and felt it would be a great asset to have such a person on my side.

Her house was a handsome one. She and her friend, Elsa Forbes, an art student, had the whole of it. It was not just a walk-up like Elma's.

When she read "My Friend Flicka," she said, "I've been saying it was time for another *Black Beauty*. You've written it."

It cannot be that she was poker-faced too, but trying to remember her with a smile on her face, I cannot. But before my lecture course ended she had sold two of my stories, one to *McCall's*, one to *Good Housekeeping*, at five hundred dollars each. She held out ten percent for her commission, though we had as yet nothing more than a friendly understanding that she would be my agent. She said that was all that was necessary.

There was an argument among Whit's coeditors about "My Friend Flicka." Some felt it was too syrupy. But Whit prevailed and one day he handed me the check for twenty-five dollars and said it would come out in the next issue.

There was some writing on the back of the check above where I would sign my name so I showed it to Sidney. Without a word, she crossed off all Whit's writing. She mailed the check back to him.

He met me in the hall one day and stopped me. If I could have understood what his long harangue was at the time, I would record it now, but it was Greek to me, except for something to the effect that I would "spoil everything."

Then, brightening up a little, he concluded, "So I'll send you another check with the same writing on the back."

He did. And again I showed it to Sidney, saying, "Let's not bother about the twenty-five dollar check. If he asks me why I haven't cashed it, I'll tell him I'm keeping it as a memento. Going to frame it and hang it on my wall."

So I had met and foiled one vulture. Who would have dreamed that it would be the very man who was opening the door for me in publishing, and who, actually, I would be going to for help for many years to come.

Just before college opened in the fall, Sidney gave a party for me. I met editors, writers, famous names, teachers, and professors. Whit sat down beside Sidney at her desk and she told him what I had said about the check.

He answered, "Of course, you've been quite right about it. If she had signed that check I would have had half of all the anthology rights."

He gave her a new check for me, with a clean back— nothing written on it.

I went home to the ranch and Helge with nine hundred and twenty-five dollars, knowing that other sales were pending, knowing, in fact, that I had broken through at last.

Thereafter, when I crossed the continent, or the east or west section of it, I no longer traveled by bus, I went by train. And in a parlor car.

28

Lippincott Publishing Company

The next year I was invited to lunch at the Ritz Hotel in New York with Whit Burnett and two members of the Lippincott Publishing Company. It was customary for a literary man to be associated with a publishing firm to help in selection of books, to work with the authors, to act as senior editor. Whit Burnett was the literary man associated with the Lippincott Publishing Company.

Lippincott was a Philadelphia firm distinguished by a long history of success, the wealth of the founders and the social prominence of the two brothers—Jo and Bertram—who were managing it now. Jo was the publisher, and hired the employees. Bertram, the younger brother, was the story scout and had more insight into the story material. He stuttered a little. George Stevens was their managing editor and had been engaged by Jo.

After "My Friend Flicka" had been published in *Story*, Whit had sent it to the juvenile department at Lippincott's, which published short stories. There, Bertram had come across it and fallen in love with it.

It was Bertram, Whit Burnett, and George Stevens who invited me to lunch that day at the Ritz. The purpose of the lunch was to persuade me to make the story into a full-length novel. Then Lippincott would publish it.

George Stevens hoped to tie me up with a contract that day. But I wouldn't consider it for a minute. I had always said (and firmly believed) that only gods and goddesses wrote novels. I didn't take their suggestion seriously, insisting that I knew my limits, I was just a short-story writer.

"But a novel would be just a succession of stories—one for each chapter."

I laughed.

"Anyway, if you got stuck, we'd all gather around you and help." This was from Whit.

George Stevens said, "We'll give you an advance on royalty. How much would you like? Three hundred? Four? Five?"

I did not laugh at that. I scorned it. "Do you imagine I would take an advance on something I myself don't believe I can do?"

As we talked I was thinking. Was there really a novel—three hundred pages of writing—in my little story? Because I had been so trained in the movies to build scenes at the drop of a hat when a director needed them, I began to see all the things that lay behind the little story which would be right and proper for a novel.

I liked Bertram Lippincott very much.

He said, "I liked your little story because it's s-s-so sentimental."

Whit looked around anxiously and shushed him. "Don't let anyone hear you say that."

Bert came back with, "D-D-Dickens was s-s-sentimental and he did pretty well too."

When the waiter brought the check, I told them that I would try. I would think it over for a week, see if the little story would expand into a big one, and let them know.

As we walked out of the dining room, Bertram was beside me. He was a big fellow, broad-shouldered, six feet tall. I was used to tall men. I looked at him and he smiled. He *could* smile. I smiled too and remembered that when Kay was a tiny boy he made up a name for me—Smiley-Face. If that book was ever to be written, I thought, a few smiles would help.

During that week of trial I put the little Corona on my lap, slipped a sheet of paper in and commanded it to "just begin with the little boy on a horse and spin away—let's see how many pages of the novel you can write."

The result was conclusive. When I stopped writing I had written fifty pages, and had not made a dent in the story yet.

So I wrote that novel. It took a year.

It's not an easy thing to write a novel. In fact it is unbelievably difficult. Over and over again I had to ask Whit to get me out of a jam. I would get into a scene and not be able to get out. In a movie you would simply write *lap, dissolve* or *cut.* How does one do it in a novel?

But Whit said, "Don't hesitate. Explain it as flatly as if it came out of the dictionary."

Lippincott brought the book out in 1941 with a modest printing of five thousand copies. They invited twenty of the best-known critics to meet the authoress at a luncheon—all twenty critics accepted and came. (A record, said George Stevens.)

"Can I believe my eyes and ears," said one critic. "You don't look or sound western at all."

At that time, the plain black silk dress was the thing to wear. I counted on my figure and the perfect cut and fit to feel smart. I answered him, "If I were a westerner would I write about the West the way I do?"

Another demanded, "Is it really your first novel? First novels are not like this."

I assured him it was.

"How did you learn to write?" he asked.

"I learned in the movies."

There was a chorus of protest. "In the movies you don't learn how to write, you learn how not to write."

I stood up for the movies. "You learn how to let the story unfold before your eyes scene after scene."

A man came up behind me—I think his name was Canby—and said, "I think you should write a novel about a wildcat."

Their written reviews came out shortly afterwards. I remember some of them. "This novel is as good as everyone says it is." "A good little story." "You won't put it down till you've finished it."

Then the fan mail began to come in. That was close to forty years ago, but it is still coming. If I had kept it all it would have filled several barrels.

Of course Helge came on to share the fun. Our happy marriage—twenty years of it now—had been put through plenty of misery at the ranch, but here was luxury. We stayed at a good hotel. Invitations poured in.

Helge was immensely popular. And how he enjoyed it! He took all the bows. He did everything but wear the orchids. He really was better suited to this acclaim than I. My reserve or shyness, or whatever it was, held me back, but it did my heart good to see his enjoyment.

The book was on the best-seller list, and the first printing exhausted in no time. I don't know how many printings there were in the first year. Next the foreign translations began, and eventually it was published in fourteen foreign editions.

I had found out now that you don't have to be a goddess to write a novel. In fact, anyone can write one provided they have sufficient imagination, perseverance, and know-how—that is, if they also understand human nature. If they don't, their characters won't ring true, and that would spoil any book. I was sure I had learned that by being a sort of father confessor to everyone since I was a child. I don't know why, but people poured out their troubles to me, sometimes their sins—even heinous sins.

The Lippincotts kept asking me for a sequel to *Flicka*. Why not? I wrote *Thunderhead,* then *Green Grass of Wyoming* and they were as successful as *Flicka*.

The Lippincotts, being publishers, were, by Joe Blakeman's definition, vultures. But the term did not fit them. Bert and his wife, Elsie, became warm and enduring friends of mine. I have visited them at their beautiful home in Philadelphia, as well as at their farm at Penllyn, Pennsylvania, and at Jamestown, Rhode Island. They were the opposite of what Papa called *hoi polloi,* and their friends gave me an entree to more social life than was compatible to me.

When Helge and I sold the ranch we bought land in Santa Barbara, California, and settled down to the job of turning that wreckage of a place into a home.

29

Wreckage

On the whole long coast-line of California there is no more attractive spot than Santa Barbara. It clings to the sea. There are just a few miles, a sort of shelf of fairly level land to hold villages, country estates, and ranches, before the wall of mountains springs up. Perhaps its known exclusiveness is to some extent the result of the fact that there simply is not room for many there.

We had bought about a hundred acres, the back part of which was a farm running up into the mountains with a Mexican farmer and his family already installed; and in the front of the lot there was the wreckage of a ranch house with a tree growing up through the floor to the ceiling and through the roof.

How charming a dwelling Helge made of that I cannot adequately describe. We had the prettiest living room, I think, which I ever had, for all the back windows opened on a small grassed lawn where we had our breakfast every morning. Our privacy was guarded by a wooded bank beyond the lawn. It rose quite high above the house.

Helge and I had been married now twenty-five years. This was the happy marriage. It was the true, the great love.

But what anguish had been enmeshed in the love—anguish, because I had actually come to doubt his truthfulness. I had been sure of one lie at the beginning, convinced that he wanted to hide some fact of his past from me, but I had decided to ignore it, unwilling to let it overshadow our union. But there were other doubts that had crept in later. He lied carelessly about little things. What about his physical faithfulness to me? He would never lie about that, would he?

It began on just that point.

Long ago at the ranch, I was emptying the pockets of his jacket before taking it to the cleaners and came upon an open letter signed by one Mabelle. It was short. "Yes. We have each other and always will have. I love you! I love you! I love you!" I had it out with Helge.

To my amazement he denied any wrongdoing and was shocked and angry at my belief that he could have "distributed himself" around. The girl had a voice, a great, big, gorgeous voice. He was trying to help her develop it, find the right teachers, and gain sufficient confidence to try for the Metropolitan Opera.

He brought her to the ranch in order that she would have the advantage of knowing me, associating with me. Helge hoped I could help him with her. This friendship had been going on a long time.

I was horrified to realize that I did not believe him. To consider him capable of poisoning a marriage with lies, so that eventually all faith would be killed—surely such doubt must be the terrible undying worm of which the Bible warns. I flung my disbelief away! I *would* believe in him!

But the worm was there, gnawing.

I suffered terribly, Helge and I were estranged for

months. Fearful tremors shook me. Was our happy marriage falling like a house of cards?

Whether or not it was an innocent affair his focus altered. It was no longer exclusively on me. In spite of what he said, he was, to use his own term, distributing himself around.

I lectured myself, told myself that in most European countries it is expected that a man will have a mistress as well as a wife. (But not, something within me wailed, when it is the great love. The true love. Two people looking honestly into each other's eyes, promising union and passion and fidelity.)

There rang in my ears the scornful remark of a Britisher, "They married for love, like servants."

Yes, we had done that. It was the only way I could marry. I would never, knowingly, share a man with another woman. I'd rather go alone.

Helge tried to explain himself to me. He had always had these friendships. Find some outstanding girl who needed someone to help her realize her potentialities. He would be the one to give her a helping hand, in a way take charge of her.

"I would know that she needed me. You see, Mary, you don't need me—you are so complete without me."

Not need him? His sociability made up for my shyness. His gregariousness offset my aloneness. His volubility complemented my silence and reserve. Above all, I needed the possessive clasp of his arms around me, declaring, "I'll never give you up."

Many other such friendships followed, all rather similar. I will say he always picked the nicest girls, and always brought them to me. I always liked them and they me, in fact they almost seemed to develop a crush on me.

There was one who, when I remonstrated with her about the impropriety of being seen so much with my husband that she was getting herself talked about, answered, "Oh, I adore him. He's my father and mother, my uncle and brother, and my best girl friend." (That was Jennie Morse.)

And we both burst out laughing.

When I asked her where she met him she said it was in the coffee shop at the hotel. They could not have been in a more public place.

Being half convinced, yet never wholly, was an old story to me now. It was after that I decided to sound out Father Meehan.

Helge never attended church with me, but had ingratiated himself with the pastor by remodeling part of a building for him. The old Irish priest was proud of me too, the author of a famous book. He was on intimate terms in our house and often had dinner with us.

One evening when I was alone with him, I asked him if he had heard any sort of unpleasant talk about Helge. He answered that everybody knew about the affair because Helge made no effort to conceal it. He described how Helge and Jennie had sat on the curb beside each other to watch the parade the other day; and at the counter of the ice cream parlor, on both occasions with Helge's arm around her.

"He flaunts it," said Father Meehan. "And at the hour when everyone in town goes to the bathing beach he is there with her. Takes her hand. They run up the beach together."

I felt as if something was squeezing my heart. Helge in his bathing trunks, running up the beach, hand in hand with Jennie. Even in Balzac and books about French intrigues, the marriage must be protected. Indiscretion was the sin, Helge knew that. This might even be proof of his innocence.

On a sudden impulse I drove down to Los Angeles and on to Arcadia and poured out my troubles to Mr. Burnell ending with, "So you see, he *may* be innocent."

Mr. Burnell agreed sardonically. "I see. What do you intend to do?"

"What do you think I should do?"

"Divorce him."

(A second divorce! How horrible!)

"Isn't it true that when there is real love in a situation, if you just hold on, don't give up too soon, it can all come out right?"

"You've held on twenty-five years," he said dryly.

Then he suddenly almost shouted, "He'll kill you!"

I was appalled. I could not take lightly anything Mr. Burnell said, and this made no sense. I knew that he and Helge had always disliked each other. At first sight enmity had flared between them. But that was long ago and should have been forgotten by now. Evidently it was not.

I drove back to Los Angeles feeling pressures on all sides of me, as if I was trapped.

I lunched in Los Angeles, then telephoned Fanny Fraser. She was home and wanted me to come right over and spend the night. The Frasers always had company, but I was in no mood for small talk so I begged off. She understood immediately.

"There will be just the three of us, Molly. Just you and Owen and me."

A warm wave of comfort flowed over me. Such good friends, these two, and from way back. I went. They gave me two big hugs. I had one drink, then another, followed by wine with the dinner, I don't know how much.

There was nothing I could tell them that they didn't already know. Los Angeles seemed as much interested in this affair as Santa Barbara, and knew all about it. All my friends were asking, "What's Molly going to do?"

The Frasers asked me the same thing.

I replied, "I can't do anything until I'm sure."

"Aren't you sure?"

"No. How can one be? There's no sure proof."

"Yes, there is." It was Fanny who told me. "It's a daytime affair. From the coffee shop they go up in the elevator to a bedroom and spend hours there. The chamber maids talk about the state they leave the bed in. Now you know."

It hit me like a sledgehammer. I said nothing, but lifted my glass and began to drink.

The blow had blotted out all thought. When dinner was over, I got to my room, undressed and went to bed. I was awakened about midnight by a terrible sound, the sobs and cries of some woman who was there in the room.

Fanny and Owen were there too. Owen closed the windows to keep the sound from the neighbors. Fanny was trying to make me swallow some capsules. I realized at last it was I myself crying so terribly, but I could not stop. I had drunk what was, for me, a good deal, but this was not drunkenness. It was an uncontrollable hysteria which continued until nearly four o'clock when Owen brought someone else into the room who gave me a hypodermic injection.

The room was quiet at last.

I awoke about eight, remembering everything. Fanny and the maid were in the room, talking softly. When they saw I was awake they came to the bed. Fanny helped me get up and bathe, brought me a clean nightgown while the maid freshened the bed, then went for the breakfast tray.

I stayed with the Frasers several days more. We drove about, met people, went to the theater. Physically I still felt very weak, as if I was just beginning to recover from a long illness. What had happened now seemed in the far distant past.

But now I knew what Mr. Burnell had meant when he said, "He'll kill you!" Something was dead in me.

When I left the Frasers to come home, it was a beautiful starlit night. From Los Angeles to Santa Barbara on the Coast Highway was about sixty miles, nothing of a drive. I just loafed along, communing with my heavenly Father.

"Thy will be done."

After all, what did it amount to? Once, it was me Helge loved and wanted. Now it was Jennie. What a trite old story. I wondered—did those two actually want to get married? It was proverbial that older men wanted younger women, so probably he did. But what about her? Perhaps she did too, for women of any age were fascinated by Helge.

I had the road practically to myself. The night was passing. My life, such as was left of it, was in God's hands.

When I got home I was an unintentional eavesdropper to a scene between Jennie's two elder brothers and Helge. They had called upon him to request that he cease his attentions to their sister. No more meetings in the coffee shop—it was getting her talked about.

I was glad it was ended, but almost sorry for Helge's humiliation. Jennie herself went off on a visit to Nevada, and her parents, a charming couple, paid a social call upon me. They talked enthusiastically about my books. Mr. Morse discussed the characters by name as if he knew them intimately. Mrs. Morse, a talented pianist, spied "Wind Harp" on the piano rack, sat down and played it brilliantly, at sight.

To the inhabitants of Montecito, these scenes said that the affair between Jennie and Helge, if it had ever been, was now ended.

But nothing was really settled. There was the possibility that the affair would not blow over, that they were seriously in love, that Helge and I had had our day and it was finished. His manner with me was slightly absent-minded, gentle but distrait.

Jennie came back from Nevada but soon went off

again on another visit. I thought they had met but it must have been carefully arranged and I could not be sure.

Then one day Helge packed his personal effects and most of his clothes in one of the old cars on the farm and departed from our home. This was the way he answered most of my uncertainties—"desertion" in California was legal grounds for divorce.

30

The Moving Finger Writes

My second divorce was very different from my first.

The year of waiting before the final decree was hardly enough to attend to all the business affairs and to divide all that Helge and I held in common. There was no trouble about the divorce action. Helge made no defense.

I had determined to ask the judge for my maiden name. Jennie would become Mrs. Helge Sture-Vasa. I would not bear the same name. The judge consented, and from that day forth I have been Mary Alsop.

At the back of our property, near the mountains, a small triangular-shaped piece of land jutted out, and on it there had always been some adobe walls, as if someone had started to build a house. Helge had spent a good many hours of work on this, shaping it into a small house, and this was where he was living now. He had made it into a charming place. It was beautifully set with some eucalyptus and pepper trees.

I sent my piano and furniture into storage and put the

house up for sale. Helge had all that was left in Wyoming. Parcels of leased land, bank account, livestock.

I moved to Westerley, a small village just the other side of the mountains, and leased a cottage there for a year. At the end of the year the final decree would be awarded and I could leave the state. I would go east to live. Elma, Reese, and Bess all had apartments in New York, weekend cottages in Connecticut, summer places in the Berkshire Hills, Tyringham, Massachusetts. There would be a warm welcome waiting for me back home.

I decided we would cross the continent on Highway Thirty. I say "we" for I would not be alone. When I had first come to Santa Barbara I had wanted a dog to take long walks with me. I didn't want to bother training a puppy, so I went to the pound to see what they had and stood outside the cage, inspecting them.

A big dog reared up, placing his paws against the cage opposite where I stood, and as we looked at each other, his brush began to wave gently. He did not have the narrow elongated face of the overbred collie but a more naturally shaped head, broad, slightly domed with brown flecks over eyes that were almost too intelligent. He was grinning and his open mouth showed a fine set of teeth. He was full grown, but less than a year old.

He knew he was mine from the first and never forgot it as long as he lived. I bought him for five dollars and named him Kim.

I would be, from now on, one of those women I had always pitied, growing old alone. No husband to stand beside them. Never invited as a couple, the way even the animals went into the ark, but singly, for whom an escort must be found to get them to dinners and parties and then home again.

I was free of any resentment toward Helge. Hatred was, for me, the worst sin, and its lesser degrees, including grudges and dislike, were not much better.

I had once, for a short time, hated him. It was when he brought Helene, one of his first girl friends, to the ranch and wanted me to adopt her. I acceded to all his requests, then suddenly turned, and with the full consent of my will (the Catholics make a point of "consent of the will," as do judges) I launched a fierce javelin of hatred at him.

I repented quickly, withdrew my ferocity and later, when we were reconciled, confessed to him. He told me he had been in the stable, felt the overwhelming blow and sank to the ground, thinking he was about to die.

I never forgot that and never did it again. In fact, in an entirely unselfish way I still loved him and grieved for him when Jennie changed her mind and married someone else. She had gone to San Francisco to meet a liner coming in from the Orient. A group of old friends were on the ship, among them a young man to whom she had once been engaged.

It was, thought all Montecito, a marvelous joke on Helge. Jennie was now Mrs. Herman Parish. I was Mrs. Mary Alsop. There was no Mrs. Helge Sture-Vasa.

On my almost daily trips from Westerley into town for my many business appointments, I passed Helge's adobe house.

I thought of my first divorce and my first husband. He had at last found the right wife, Lucile Armstrong, and was happily married.

It seemed to me I ought to say good-bye to Kent before I left. He was the father of my children and I would never see him again. Time was getting short. So one day I telephoned him, explained and said if he would meet me at the drugstore we could have a cup of coffee together and say good-bye. But he insisted that I come to their house. He wanted me to meet Lucile.

Their house was built on top of a cliff overlooking the sea. One entered from the back. I stood at the foot of the long flight of stone steps and looked up. Kent stood at the top, a huge figure, with wide outstretched arms. I went slowly up. His big arms wrapped around me, his face was wet with tears, and I heard again those sobs I had heard so many years ago when he carried me up to my room.

Helge telephoned me one day. I recognized his voice instantly and answered gaily, "Oh, it's you! How's my boy?"

His voice dropped an octave to the deep wooing note, "My sweetheart!"

I was amazed at the way my heart jumped. It took me back. It was the voice of my lover-husband that I had heard all those happiest days of my life. I could not speak.

"I called you to ask you, Mary, if you would try it again with me?"

"And go through all this over again?"

"It wouldn't be the same. It would all be different."

"How can you imagine that I would believe anything you said?"

The guttural voice again. "I'm sorry I asked you."

But he telephoned me again.

"I heard you are going east."

"Yes."

"When?"

"As soon as my lease ends at Westerley. It won't be long now."

We discussed the trip quite as if he had some responsibility in what I did. At last he wrung out of me a promise to stop and see him at the adobe house before I left. A dangerous promise, I thought, as I hung up the phone. I knew Helge. He would get me in his arms. I knew myself.

My fine new car was packed at last. The tonneau was filled with my writing paraphernalia. Many boxes of stories. Suitcases. My tape recorder. Several typewriters. They were piled up level with the seat. I put a rug on that so Kim could lie or sit on it. The Mayfair van with the rest of my household furniture and the Mason and Hamlin grand piano would be traveling the same road, Highway Thirty.

All the good-byes had been said, and soon I was on the road that led from Westerley right past Helge's adobe house and there was no going back, for the lease was up. It was early in the morning, for I wanted to get a good start on the long ride.

If I did not stop to say good-bye to Helge, I would be in town in twenty minutes, and after the one right-angle turn to the left Kim and I would be on our way for the long crossing. But I had promised him.

Before coming to Helge's house I would pass the church and Father Meehan's rectory. I stopped there. Although I had said good-bye to Father Meehan, I would say another. I told him about my promise to Helge. And my fears that, even now, Helge would find a way to hold me.

I longed to be captured again. To feel Helge's arms around me, but I felt on the verge of a breakdown. When a woman of my age has a breakdown, what can happen? A stroke? A coronary? Something terrible! If Helge put me through this sort of thing again, I'd never survive it. And I didn't trust him.

Father Meehan, always understanding, said, "Some promises are better broken."

I sat there in his living room, my head sunk in my hands, and finally asked for paper and pencil. I wrote:

Dear,

I really did mean to stop to say good-bye to you as I promised, but when it comes to the point, I simply haven't the heart.

With love,
Mary

*   *   *

Kim and I drove straight on into town and turned left toward Highway Thirty.

There is a postscript to this chapter, for in a very short time Helge had found himself a new wife. She was an attractive young-middle-aged woman of excellent social position. It was another happy marriage, and again lasted twenty-five years, ended by Helge's death from a coronary.

A friend sent me the obituary notice. In it Helge was spoken of as a famous horseman.

PART FOUR

31

Stone Walls and Pastures

The crossing of the continent created a great chasm in my emotional landscape, splitting my life into two parts, not equal by any means, for much more lay behind me than ahead. The greatest change was leaving love behind.

I often thought I have been at fault in my loving, have been too intense. Perhaps I had been intended for a Vestal Virgin and had strayed from the path.

It was not that I did not love love. I did. There was "Wind Harp," which Mr. Spencer had called pure burning love. I had written that from my heart. And what about my children?

But there are different kinds of love. For me there would be no more "eros"; only "agape," divine love, and "filia," love of family and friends.

Before even finding a place to live, I had to connect with my family.

Elma had never married. She had held the position of college physician at Barnard College for twenty-five years. As she had started out in China writing *My Chinese Days*, she kept on writing stories. She, like me, had writing in the blood.

Bess was a widow with two children and, when I came east, was in Paris, furthering her musical career. Matrigna was in the beautiful house she and Papa had built and lived in at North East Harbor, Maine, in the summers before he died.

And Reese? Reese was now what is called a "big" lawyer, very successful, occupied mostly with the reorganization of railroads. The love and shared feelings that Reese and I had known in childhood were still there. When I sang to him the first four measures of an African war chant that had come over the radio the year before and asked him if he had noticed it, he immediately sang the last four measures. We were still on the same wavelength, our attention caught and held by the same things.

He had been married three times. His first marriage had given him four lovely children, Ba, Jim, Ann, Robert, and ended in divorce. His second, to a woman he adored, ended in her death from cancer. His third ended in his wife's death from an accidental overdose of barbituates.

He was said to be the most attractive man in New York. He was now unmarried and lived in a luxurious six-room New York apartment with Maud, a faithful and devoted colored woman to cook, clean, wait on table and in every way watch over him.

When I had gone away so many years ago, I had not been much more than the "prod," the prodigal daughter, but they had now to meet someone who was considered a celebrity. Quite a change!

I tried to decide where I would like to settle down and live. A country place, of course. But near a university because I might need the library for my writing. And near New York for its shops and because it was more *home* than any other place.

I cruised for a long time, visiting old friends, making

new ones, narrowing my search down to Connecticut, close
enough to New Haven for visits to Yale and its famous
library. And I was charmed by the countryside with its
winding, sometimes circular roads—often you came out
where you began. At every turn there was a different view,
charming homesites, with woods, hills, streams.

Between a little village called Monroe and another
called Stevenson was an old farm for sale into which the
road wound rising to a ridge. I got out of my car and
walked to the ridge and looked down. The ground fell away
slightly. If I built the house on this ridge I could look into
a distance that appeared to go for hundreds of miles.

I stood there for a long time, thinking. I already had
in mind a house plan with some definite measurements. I
wanted a living room of twenty feet by twenty feet, with
eleven-foot ceilings and many tall windows to overlook the
view.

But if you entered the house from Bagburn Road, as I
had, there must first be an entrance hall, twelve feet by
twelve feet and paved with brick because of the ice and
snow, boots and skates that would be dropped on it.

I studied the ridge. The living room would be lower
than the hall. Four steps would be needed. How charming!

To my left, and down a little, was a huge oak. Farther
down and to the right, another. A third made the points of
a triangle. I could call them Meshach, Shadrach and
Abednego.

I bought the farm, hired an architect, found a master
carpenter who was also a neighbor, Erik Olsen, and set
them to work in time to embark on a Dutch liner for
England to attend the wedding of my son with Deirdre
Lumley-Savile, the daughter of a British peer. Kent, now a
major, had met Deirdre while assigned to foreign duty in
London.

England is a horsey country. The English thought it
amazing that *My Friend Flicka,* a book about a horse,

describing not only a horse's physical attributes of speed and power but the very movements of its soul, should have been written by an American woman who wrote under the name of her Irish grandmother!

I had often visited England. Ever since we were little tots, our grandmother or someone had been taking us "abroad." But I had never before gone to England as a celebrity, to be seized, congratulated, and handed around like a plate of cookies.

On one occasion there was a meet, with a breakfast before a hunt at Gryce, the country place in Yorkshire of Lord Savile, the elder brother of my son's wife. I stood in an immense crowd of riders, horses, grooms, servants with trays, close to a huge man who was my escort. He held two big horses by the reins.

The noise, the shouting, the confusion was indescribable. I recognized some strange accents. Farmers, I knew, went on these hunts. The accents of the lords and ladies, the broad "A," the throaty gargle and the exaggerated inflections I was accustomed to, but I still found it hard to understand. There were women already mounted in the crowd. They looked quite old and wore derby hats and were on sidesaddles.

The sort of riding clothes I wore at the ranch looked just as well here. I had found a jockey cap which not only gripped my head and held my hair, but which stayed on and was becoming. My spurs were spikes about an inch and a half long driven into the heel of my boot—no rowls or clashing chains over the instep, no hard boots and breeches, but instead, soft elastic-sided shoes covered almost entirely by the long slim jodhpurs which were drawn down over them with a strap under the instep of the shoe. My whole outfit was black. Trim, indestructible, and becoming.

Suddenly there was an increase of movement and noise. A groom took the bridles of the horses my companion was holding. I saw he was about to put me on one of the horses and prepared to be mounted properly. But he just lifted me in both hands and put me up on that hunter's back, gave me the reins and climbed on the other.

I would have been safer on a sidesaddle with the pommels and a short stirrup to lock me on. My horse was far too broad for me to get any knee grip. I slid around on him and now my mental confusion gave way to a definite horror. After writing *My Friend Flicka,* to go to England and fall off the first horse they put me on.

We plunged down a bank, then up one, leaped a wall, riding like mad, as if we must get there (where?) ahead of everyone else. I stayed on, but at the expense of such fierce concentration as would have written me another book.

Of that short visit to horsey England, the thing I remember best is not the confusion, the noise, the wild ride—but the width of my horse's back. In spite of it, I stayed on.

During the war England had been full of young American servicemen, and the newspapers printed the gripes of young Britishers: "They're over paid. They're over sexed. And they're over here!"

Wanting to find out if anyone in England liked Americans, I asked the chambermaids at the Grosvenor Hotel where I was staying and got these answers:

"They're smashing!"

"They can do anything!"

"And they're *kind.*"

On this side of the water, when I got home, I asked the same question of the small cabby who carried my bags and had just returned from England. He was still wearing his uniform blouse. He answered sadly, "They ain't got no respek for us."

I worried about my grandchildren to be.

On the ship coming home I had been obliged to share a cabin with Mrs. Richard Flint and her daughters. This happenchance gave me one of my dearest friends. They lived in New Haven and we had barely got home before she gave me a big tea, to meet everyone worth knowing in New Haven. When they asked where it was that I was building my home, I said, "On a back road. With stone walls and pastures." It was well hidden. No one would guess such a place could be tucked away there.

I had had time now to think of a suitable name for my new home. Tyrawley was the name of a property our ancestors had owned in Ireland. I named it that.

Meanwhile the building was progressing. Stone masons were erecting the two big chimneys which embraced the central block of the house, from which two wings continued along the ridge. What I needed now was a place to live in while my house was being finished, and I found it in Monroe Center.

Monroe Center was located on a typical New England green. A dozen ancient elms with an occasional bench underneath left plenty of space for baseball games Saturday afternoons. It was ringed around by the town's vital organs. A small, white steepled church at each end, rectories— beautiful old houses made of brick—the firehouse, the library, the police station, the offices of Charles Covert, the lawyer, and Dr. Williams, the health officer. (The last two would become my lawyer and doctor, and never did I have better.)

The Russel Masons had bought one of the old houses and made the top floor into a separate apartment which they rented. It happened to be vacant now. Kim and I moved in and were comfortably settled for the duration.

Whatever else I did, I never stopped writing. No matter where I went, my portable went with me, as well as a big accordion case with a half-written story or sketches for a book, or outlines or whole scenes in every slot.

Peggy Mason constituted herself the guardian of my visiting list. Peggy had started out as a trained nurse; she was an RN, but had switched to real estate and was now buying and selling farms and real estate all over New England. She had a talent for protocol, which was as active here as it is everywhere. My new friends were Charles and Katharine Covert, Warren and Helen Drouet, Dot and Phil Gossler, Marian and Graham Patmore. All were interested in antiques, in buying, remodeling and selling old houses. Dot and Katharine were professional interior decorators. Marian Patmore was a famous photographer. The Drouets raised chickens on their place. These warm and hospitable people have remained my friends ever since.

We often gave each other little keepsakes. Dot knitted for me the Christmas stocking I would soon be needing for a grandchild, thick wool, red, green, and white. I gave a muzzle to Warren Drouet for his great Dane, Bounder, who chewed up so many little dogs on his morning rounds that Helen was worried sick. Helen had implored Warren to take Bounder on a leash, but Warren would not. As there was no shop, not even Abercrombie and Fitch in New York, which had a muzzle big enough for Bounder, I undertook the project—I had the design of Kim's, who was also a biter, to go by. I don't know how many weeks I sat on the floor in the Drouet living room, with large pieces of special leather (for which I had scoured the state), tape measure, scissors, boxes of small steel studs, and a tool to fasten them at the juncture. Bounder stood proudly beside me, enjoying the fittings and being the center of attention. When it was finished and Warren, in the mornings, would shake it at Bounder, the dog would run to thrust his head into it, so everyone was happy. Bounder is long since deceased, but that muzzle hangs on a nail in Warren's fireplace, looking, so an artist said, like the work of a sculptor.

The keepsake I remember the best was given me by the Patmores, who specialized in cats—they had a couple of dozen. One evening when I was dining with them, they picked out a calico cat and gave her to me. I still have her progeny.

Tyrawley was ready to live in at last. Clean, polished, the furniture placed, the curtains hung. An archway separated the living room from the small area that would be called the music room. The piano stood with dignity in the small area, glass all around it.

In future years, when I sat on the bench, playing, by twisting my head around I could see my brother Reese when he was visiting, sitting in the small sunny patio I had made especially for him, reading Trollope, his favorite author. Sometimes he would put his book down, lean his head back against his easy chair and listen to me playing "Wind Harp."

When Reese was seventy he was under a doctor's care for high blood pressure. Planning a visit to his country place in Tyringham, he was told he must first come to the hospital for a checkup.

Everything was favorable and he packed his bag and began to dress. As he stood, buttoning up his vest, his heart suddenly stopped beating. After a moment or two he slowly sank to the floor.

So there was another separation for Reese and me. Perhaps it will be a long one. But separation cannot take him from me, for he is part of me.

I play a piece on the piano, first softly, then "big." I am smiling. I strike a particularly lovely chord and say, "Hear that, Reese?"

I was lying in my narrow, antique walnut bed at the other end of the house when the telephone rang. It was Kent calling from London. "He's got ten little fingers and ten little toes." And so was born my first grandson, Jonathan. I did not sleep again that night.

I thought of the upstairs of my house, planned for just

such a contingency: divided in two, one part sunny bedroom and bath for a general houseworker (she was destined to be Bertha, who stayed with me for many years), and the other part double bedroom, spare room, bathroom, and sundeck for Kent, Deirdre, and the baby.

At dawn I got up and looked out the window. There was a stone wall between Tyrawley and Bagburn Road, and a fox was walking slowly along it, its full brush sloping down gracefully. I was elated. Here I was in the country which I had always so loved, and a wild animal right outside my window headed for the woods on the left, also my property, in which, no doubt, many wild animals sheltered.

Once a year I had a party at Tyrawley which was just for our family connections—about sixty persons. A luncheon—cold ham, salad of stuffed eggs on watercress, a delicious hot casserole of mushrooms and rice and blueberry pie. After lunch the young ones dove for quarters in the big swimming pool, and later on the lawn showed what they could do in the way of acrobatics—back flips, front flips, cartwheels, head stands. The largest contingent at the party came down from Tyringham, Massachusetts. The smallest, up from Washington. There were also two lovely girls from England, Reese's granddaughters. His eldest daughter had married an Englishman, Henry Howard. Kent and my nephew Edward ran the show.

I let nothing interfere with my work routine. I did my writing in the first hours of the morning when my mind was fresh and uncluttered by anything else. No newspapers came to the house. By four o'clock in the morning I was in the kitchen brewing myself that first delicious cup of coffee. I would be warmly dressed in black jersey trousers and black cotton artist's smock. I would have had a cold bath, doing my simple sit-up exercises while the tub filled. I would have turned up the oil burner, which shared the

basement with Kim and a set of wash tubs. Notes were
ready and waiting on my desk to begin. These had been
prepared the evening before. If I had dined out it was with
the understanding that I could eat and run without saying
good night to my hostess. I would just disappear and slip
out a back door to my car. So by the time I took the first
break at ten for a hearty breakfast, a good deal had been
done. After that I wrote steadily until I was so exhausted I
could not speak or recognize what I was looking at.

What would rest me then was to get in my car and
drive slowly along the beautiful roads, looking at the
wayside trees, paying special attention to the shapes of the
leaves, all differing, oak leaves or tulip or maple or beech.

The remainder of the afternoon was filled with errands
and visits. Everyone knew me and seemed to be proud to
have me in their midst. They had named their horses, if
they had horses, after the horses in my books.

When asked the secret of my success, I translate the
word *amateur:* "I am motivated by love. "My son, Kent,
explains it more blatantly: "She works like h__!" People
would stop me in the shops or on the streets to talk to me
about life, as if I ought to know the answers to their
questions.

"Is the game worth the candle?" asked the butcher,
one of a couple of fine young Scandinavians. When I
answered, "About ten percent is," he was delighted and
told his brother.

"Look for the ten percent," he would say.

Kent and Deirdre had another boy, Richard Halifax,
who, until he was two years old, looked exactly like
Winston Churchill. In other words he was so homely I felt
guilty and ashamed when I told his parents he was
beautiful. But my words were prophetic. At five, he was as
handsome a boy as I have ever laid eyes on.

At Tyrawley one summer my oculist, Dr. Stow,

completed his yearly examination of my eyes, and pushed back to me across the table the same reading glasses I had been wearing, saying that stronger ones would be no help to me any longer. I had been a voracious reader all my life, usually finishing a book of average length at one sitting. How precious to me were those hours of escape!

I tried the Bates method set forth in the book *Better Vision Without Glasses,* but that not quite impenetrable veil which lay between me and every object I looked at was still there. I settled at last for the talking books, and the little transistor radios which were a boon to the nearly blind and nearly deaf. Though these offered news, music, gossip, and stories, only a small percentage of world events reached me. More and more I looked inward for sights and sounds that were keen and bright with color and interest.

I began to think about those things I had always intended to do but so far had not even started. One of those was the writing of a musical. As I had the two gifts, composing and story-writing, I was a natural for it, like Noel Coward and Cole Porter. Since childhood I had been carrying around with me a big box labeled "For the Musical," putting into it all themes and melodies which seemed to me suitable for stage songs and dances. I also had ideas for the story, but not yet in shape so it could be written.

Another thing I'd always intended to do was to write a book that was about people, not horses. There was a good deal about this in my big accordion notebook. The idea I set down here—that there might be certain women intended to be Vestal Virgins—had so intrigued me that I kept thinking about it. Suppose the protagonist was a man rather than a woman. Suppose he was a religious, perhaps a true mystic. Perhaps he fell in love with a siren and got married; his divine and his human love would pull him in opposite directions.

This big novel, with the title *The Son of Adam*   .

Wyngate, was the first major piece of writing I produced at Tyrawley. J. B. Lippincott rejected the book, a new experience for me. I offered it to McKay, who accepted it, and it climbed to near the top of the best-seller list.

Kent was now in Holland at the Air Defense Technical Center, and I went over to visit them there. It was in Holland that my third grandchild, Barbara, was born seven years after Richard.

Barely had I finished writing *The Son of Adam Wyngate* and the book which followed it, *Novel in the Making,* which was about the art of writing a book, than Kent was back in this country with his family. In the course of time, they settled into a house they already owned in Washington, only a seven-hour run from Tyrawley. I immediately rented a small furnished house in Washington. Tyrawley was formidable in winter—I decided that I would spend my winters in Washington near them.

Kent and Deirdre brought Barbara to Tyrawley before she was a year old. If you had visited Tyrawley at that time and stood outside the dining room window looking in at a big clothes basket which rested on a bench there, you might have seen hovering over it a baby's naked foot about the size of a mouse. This would have been your introduction to Barbara, named after an ancestor, the Countess of Scarbrough.

Barbara measured up to what was expected of any female of her lineage in the way of beauty, but she had more than beauty. Now that she is entering this autobiography, I will let her speak for herself.

When she was three I, entranced by her baby talk, could not resist the temptation to mimic, and said, "So you liked your Klistmas presents?"

She fastened her blue eyes on me and admonished me gravely, "Hydie, I are trying very hard to say my words right, but you are a big lady."

I was properly abashed.

*   *   *

Another book came out of the Tyrawley years. I don't know how long I had been there when, cleaning out a closet one day, I came upon a sizable manuscript which I had completely forgotten. Opening the first page I saw that it was the diary of a summer at the ranch. Standing there I turned page after page without moving. A long time later I turned the last page.

I had found a treasure. I gave it the title *Wyoming Summer,* and it was published by Doubleday.

When Kent was in Holland he had written me that, since costs were so high in America, would it not be a good idea to have recordings made in Holland of songs and dances of the musical? I could then use them as samples. Play them to people. Play them around. This worked out well and he became vitally interested in promoting the show. What an agent! He had a talent for it. He was an entrepreneur!

Having recovered my family again, an augmented family, and caught up on all they had to tell me, made this part of my life really glamorous.

In addition to babies or children and family affairs to talk about, we had the musical. I had the big box of songs and dances. We had the sample records that had been made in Holland. But that indispensable glue which binds all together—the background music, the little links and arrows, pushing and pulling, giving it all the desired shape—was lacking.

That word *glue,* so apt and telling, is not original with me. I had read it in a book on the writing of musicals. It signified the very stuff that was now needed to complete my work. I was sure there must be somewhere a teacher who could teach me how to find the glue. There was.

I was in church in Washington one Sunday, a large and important church, and still thinking disconsolately about these things when I began to listen to the roulades which came from an organ played in the upper gallery at the back of the church.

If I had been praying I would have said it was an answer to prayer. Organists are thorough musicians.

I waited at the back of the church until the organist came down from the gallery and then asked him if he ever gave lessons in harmony.

His smiling answer, "For twenty-five years at Catholic University."

So began my many years of study with Conrad Bernier.

I had two homes now, Washington and Tyrawley, and drove back and forth as occasion demanded.

So much that I had planned and hoped for had come to pass. But the musical was still more dream than reality. More a childish wish. A promise to myself? Perhaps. At least a promise to try, for the trying would be fun, win or lose.

One day, in New York, I signed an important contract with the Sam Fox Music Publishing Company and realized as I was driving home that, for once, I had nothing cooking. My decks were cleared for action. I might start the musical in earnest now—at least write the play. I had told the story many times to get reader reaction, and changed it a little every time I told it. For the stage it must be exact. No more changes.

Was I ready to put it on paper? If not, I challenged myself, you never will be. You've just been playing with the idea all these years. A pipe dream. Give it up.

Suddenly I was full of determination, the conclusive factor for me, for that meant never giving up.

I began to think of the Wyoming ranch and the sheep and those funny sheepherders. They could be my funny men. I thought of the one old sheepherder who had lost his grandson and spent a lifetime looking for him.

As I entered the Tyrawley driveway, I thought of the boy and girl romance, the boy the lost grandson, of course; the girl, the beautiful daughter of the ranch owner.

As I entered my subterranean garage and shut off my engine, suddenly I had a lyric—the mother warning them not to elope.

If you're off on your own,
Starting life all alone,
There'll be an ache in your heart,
Perhaps forever.

I always know when story material that boils up in me is "hot" or tepid. This was hot, and before I took my things off, I went through the house to my small writing room and jotted down what had come to me. I amplified it the next day. In a week I had a complete outline of the play.

To write a play was not hard for me, though all my experience had been with screen plays. I knew all about plot, characters, and dialogue.

At last I had it, the complete written play, every spoken word, every action described exactly, as well as a collection of lyrics (if I needed more I could write them). My way of writing was to sit at the piano, the long pad of yellow paper to the right for lyrics, and a block of music score paper on the left. I wrote the songs, words and music, practically together, and they sounded like that. Anyone could read it now, visualize the action, judge the story as easily as if it were a book.

I hoped I could get Louise Sillcox to read it. She was executive secretary of the Authors League, to which I belonged. She was a top authority.

I sent her the script, waited a few days, then telephoned her. We chatted a few moments. Yes, she had had time to read it. Yes, she thought she could recommend a theatrical agent. I would need a good agent.

"But do tell me what you thought of it."

There was a little pause, then, as if blurting it out, her amazing answer, "Crazy about it."

"What particularly?"

"Your whole approach."

She got me the agent considered the best in the business, Harold Friedman.

I had a meeting with Friedman but he was discouraging. It was an original, written directly for the stage. Just what the theatrical theorists have been urging for years. But no producer wants an original.

"If your musical had been taken from a published best-seller like *Anna and the King of Siam,* people all over the country would have been talking about it for years."

He had other objections. I had done it all myself so he had no big names to sell. "The fact that you are a celebrity in the literary world has no bearing here; they've never heard of you."

I defended not myself but my work. "People like it. Story and music."

He shrugged. "Perhaps it has merit. I'll take your word for it. But merit will never get you a producer."

But it did. Not one of the big professional producers who have a half a million dollars to spend, but a university, the music department of the Catholic University of America, where I had been studying with Conrad Bernier.

I had not yet decided on a title. At a party a woman reporter asked me where it was set, and I, weary of continual harping on bygone achievements, said, "Oh, Wyoming, of course."

The reporter enthused, *"Oh, Wyoming!* Sheer genius, Miss O'Hara! Oh, Wyoming!"

So it opened with that title at C.U. They gave us a four-day production under the baton of Dr. John Paul, and I maintain it was a great success, though the drama department, natural enemy of the music department, slammed it with nasty reviews, some of them written even before the first performance took place. The animus seemed directed against me personally—I must be a snooty stuck-up person to imagine that because I was a celebrity in the literary field that meant I could write a musical.

But at one of the performances there was present an out-of-town reporter who wrote a review which said, "Praise of the music was unanimous."

We had hoped and thought that some big producer would be so charmed by our show he would grab it. This had not happened. But that one good review got into the newspapers and was widely quoted. General opinion agreed with him.

The faculty at C.U. thought that if it could be put on elsewhere in the country on the occasion of some big festival that would help greatly. I thought of the week-long festival in Cheyenne, Wyoming, named Frontier Days, which featured tough riding, bronco busting and everything that was western. Thousands of visitors came to see this. And, after all, was not my story a Cheyenne story? It seemed a natural.

The town had a good theater, accommodating one thousand people. Our crowd at C.U. was eager to go. The cost would be considerable, but Markane Company, the company Kent and I had formed, thought it a good way to dispense the royalties from *Flicka,* which continued to roll in.

I entered into correspondence with Remington Berry, who owned the theater. Finally the deal was closed. We rented the theater.

32

The Catch Colt

As everyone knows, musicals do not achieve their final shape until they have had a number of tryouts. Cheyenne was our second tryout, and after the opening performance, we were eager to see what audience reactions were.

The day after the opening, I was walking down the street and a group of women got out of a Texas limousine and clustered around me. "Aren't you Miss O'Hara? We saw your show last night. It is simply magnificent! If we were going to stay on, we'd go every night."

At the theater after the show a woman exclaimed to her husband, who had come to pick her up, "You missed it! What a show!" And later in the week's run, Mr. Remington Berry himself said, "I always go home as early as I can when the evening show starts and leave it to the boys to close up, but not with this show. I stay to the very end, so I won't miss one note of that last chorus."

I had received a polite letter from the organization of Wyoming Newspaper Women asking me to be the guest of honor at lunch at the Plains Hotel Wednesday following the opening of the play.

I had accepted their invitation, envisioning a little affair of eight ·or ten people, given perhaps in the coffee shop of the Plains Hotel, a cozy place to lunch.

The luncheon was not in the coffee shop but in the big ballroom. It would have held an army. It was full of small tables at which the newswomen sat, and the back of the room and the two sides was standing room only, occupied mostly by men. Even this was not the entire audience: We were hooked up to England and France.

Wyoming is four hundred miles square. The big buses that brought these reporters must have left the four corners of the state before sunrise, picking up their passengers at every village.

I had been very careful about my costume, remembering that a group of women would be scrutinizing me. Gimlet eyes. When I was dressed I went to a long mirror and looked myself over. Only a youthful figure could wear so plain a dress, a cotton print, a white background, different shades of gray patterned in bold sheaves over it. The skirt was slightly bouffant. The weather was sizzling hot so my face and neck, arms and legs were bare and sunburned. I was sure I looked about twenty-five years younger than I really was.

At the luncheon I stood on a dais before a microphone. I was to talk about the show and answer any questions. The question and answer session had been going on some time when a newspaper man yelled from the back, "But what about the title, Miss O'Hara? It opened in Washington with the title *Oh, Wyoming!* Here it's billed as *Top O' the Big Hill*."

Actually this was the result of a sudden inspiration on my part. The transcontinental trainmen have a name for the Rockies. They call them the Big Hill. This so pleased me that I composed a march ending with "two locomotives to the top of the big hill."

"I'm glad this came up," I said. "I'd like a consensus on this. Which one do you like best? Two other titles have also been suggested: *Boy Meets Girl* and *The Catch Colt*."

Responses came from all over the room. The loudest was for *The Catch Colt*.

As I left the hall I was accosted by a newswoman, notebook and pencil in hand. "Your age, please, Miss O'Hara?"

"I never tell it," I answered smiling.

"People want to know," she insisted.

I smiled again but closed my lips.

"Then I'll get it any way," she threatened.

We eyed each other. I sighed and said, "Seventy-one."

Every one of the five days we had still to run taught me much. I saw that I would practically have to rewrite the show. But that, I had heard, was the usual thing. No artist considers time when working in his own particular field. You use as much time as is needed. There is always plenty more.

After the last performance the troupe scattered, blown away like a pile of autumn leaves.

33

The Golden Key

Neither Kent nor I nor our coproducers and friends at C.U. ever doubted that there would be another production of *The Catch Colt,* and that this time around the critics would point their thumbs up instead of down and we would have a Broadway hit after all.

The production at Cheyenne had been invaluable in showing what had to be done to bring it up to par. As soon as we reached home we got to work.

It is a truism that plays are not written, they are rewritten. I began to rewrite. The recordings of the music needed a complete going over. The musical director at Catholic University, Mike Cordovana, and I spent hours together. Alter that key. Change the range of this song. This bit of melody is hard to sing. Dr. Paul thought the pitch of the last chorus was one note too high. Eventually Mike performed the whole show again using the university students, an extraordinary assemblage of talent. This gave us a set of recordings for promotion purposes of which we could be proud.

Kent, my energetic entrepreneur, was our promoter, and sang the praises of *The Catch Colt* wherever he went. But we needed a new orchestration.

My constant listening to the good music station on the radio had acquainted me with all the orchestrators, and I wanted the best. Hershey Kay was my choice but I was told it was impossible to get him or even to reach him. All the same, we carefully packaged the fine record Mike had made of the show and sent it with a letter to Hershey Kay.

There was no reply.

When a good many weeks had passed, Kent went to New York and rang Hershey Kay's doorbell. Kent explained who he was and why he was there and Mr. Kay was rather apologetic, saying that he had been too busy to give the matter his attention.

When Kent was invited in he saw an unopened package and recognized his own handwriting. He said, "I'm just on my way back to Washington, but if you have a half hour, we could listen to that record now, and then I'll take it with me."

Mr. Kay agreed, took the record and put it on his machine.

The first measures were gay and challenging, open-air music. Then came the long swinging rhythms of a cantering horse.

The first act was on one side of the record, the second on the other side. They listened in silence. When a few numbers of the second half had been played a telephone rang somewhere and Mr. Kay stopped the record and left the room to answer it. This gave him time to think and make up his mind.

When he came back he said, "This is good."

Kent asked, "Would you be interested in making an orchestration of it?"

And Mr. Kay, evidently a man of few words, answered simply, "Yes."

This was an immense gain for us.

As soon as the financial arrangements had been completed he began on the work.

For a long time Kent had been asking me to write the play in story form. He had heard me tell it many times and always with dramatic effect. If I wrote it just as I told it, it would be published as all my stories were. That was the golden key to success and I had it right in my hands.

Of course he was right. But it is not sufficient for me to have merely the intention to write a story. I go through a process. It is not just the long mulling over of the material. I cannot begin until the story, as it were, starts to write itself.

The first sentence, a perfect first sentence, must float up. But this had not happened yet so, actually, I did not have the golden key in my hands. But one day the sentence did come.

It is always the greatest thrill when it does.

"He was what is known in Wyoming as a cow puncher. A tall, handsome fellow who thought he was about twenty. He could not be sure because he had no family to keep track of his birthdays."

I went to the typewriter and wrote that down. Then sat almost in a daze of joy while scene after scene unfolded in my mind, the meeting between those two youngsters, their helpless love and the impossible barrier that kept them apart.

Such tales are beloved by everyone.

I couldn't wait to begin. First I would buy some clothes—my Washington house was near a good shopping district. Pretty clothes always stimulated me. A new dress that was becoming actually heightened my vitality and ability. But with my failing eyesight the walk to Saks was something of an ordeal. Every street corner looked like every other street corner and that gave me no landmarks.

However, I got there and went in. Just inside the door

at Saks, to the left, was the lingerie department with a display of new boudoir accessories. Of these there was nothing I needed except a new bra.

My size was thirty-six with a B cup. There was one I liked in the right size. But I had come for a dress, not lingerie. I left that room and hunted the whole shop through but found no dress. Tired out, I went back and bought the bra and took it home with me.

I knew it would have to be altered because I am slightly larger on the right side than the left. I tried on the new bra and got a surprise. It was very snug on the left side. Then I saw why. Deep within, against my ribs, was a hard lump, about the size and shape of a small apricot.

It was a shock. There are few people nowadays who do not know all about the horrors of cancer. Once I had heard the terrible screams of a woman who lived a block away who was dying of cancer.

But more breast tumors are benign than malignant. The rate of growth is so slow when the person is over seventy, she would probably die before the tumor had time to make trouble. Another thing—they are frequently in a capsule, as if nature had arranged to keep them from spreading. What I could not bear was to be stopped now that I was launched on the new story and it was all opening before me.

I had heard all the warnings about early detection of tumors. But if I told Dr. Richwine, to whom I went every fortnight for an intravenous injection of vitamins, it would interrupt my writing with consultations, tests, a biopsy. Doctors do not dare to take chances, but *I* could. The tumor had never troubled me and probably never would. I would tell no one about it, just proceed as if nothing had happened.

My lump made no trouble, and I grew used to its being there and going everywhere with me, being my bedfellow at night. I was sure it must be in a capsule because it was so hard. When President Ford's wife, Betty Ford, was discovered to have a cancer in her breast there was much general conversation about it and I asked Dr. Richwine why, if the tumor was encapsulated, they could not leave it there permanently instead of operating. He said, "The tumor finally breaks through the capsule and sometimes even the skin."

I thought of that when, one night, my lump started itching ferociously.

I wanted to claw at it.

I explained the strange phenomenon to myself. The tumor had probably broken free of the capsule and I was alarmed lest the rest of what the doctor had described would ensue.

I would have to tell him, but I would wait until the story was finished.

Then I noticed that the shape of my lump was changing. It was no longer like an apricot, it was more like a small sickle pear, with the round part against my ribs and the pointed end almost against my skin. But they would never dare operate now on a woman my age. If they did, that would be the end of me.

That would be all right. It was long overdue and so many had gone before me: Reese, Nan Holbrook, Vernon Spencer, Mr. Burnell, Bess, the Frasers, and so many others. I had outlived them all. Besides, it is true—what they say—that the closer you come to death the more comfortable it seems.

There is a beautiful poem by Tennyson, "Crossing the Bar." I like that, wading out in the sand, deeper and deeper, then up again on to the bar, then the long low dive into the ocean. This time, no bar. No return.

I finished the story at last, revised it the usual number of times, polished it. It had taken me almost exactly two years to write. Kent packaged it and mailed it to the publisher.

So one day, when Dr. Richwine had just got the needle into my vein, I said, "Dr. Richwine, I've got a growth in my left breast. I think it's an abcess."

Without any surprise, he said quietly, "I'll finish this, then I'll examine it."

When he had done so he said, "It's not an abcess. An abcess would be soft. This is hard. I'm going to send you to Jim Boland. He's seen more of these than I have. I'll call Kent and have him take you."

"Oh, not another doctor!"

"You'll like him. He'll be the surgeon."

Dr. Richwine was already at the telephone. In ten minutes it had all been arranged. The meeting with Dr. Boland would be at his downtown office, 10:00 A.M. Thursday.

Kent drove me through the crowded streets. I was in great suspense. There were a good many people waiting in the reception room when Kent and I got there. He steered me to an easy chair and went to the desk.

As we had just come in from the blazing sunlight, the room seemed impenetrably dark. Not the faintest glimmer of light. But people were moving around freely. The darkness was in me. I felt terribly ill and thought I was going to die right then. That would settle everything.

Then I remembered Mr. Burnell's teaching. "There is a vitality which has nothing to do with the illness or health of the body."

I laid these words upon myself like a poultice, relaxed, leaned my head back and sat in my private darkness, thinking about what I should write next, perhaps the book of collected stories I had been planning for so long.

Presently the nurse came to tell us the doctor was ready. We went in and met Dr. Boland, who had already talked to Dr. Richwine. There was a little partitioned-off cubicle where he examined me. He went back and talked to Kent while the nurse put on my blouse and jacket again.

He was sitting behind his big desk when I rejoined them and he said, "Well, you have a little lump but at your age it doesn't much matter if it is malignant or not."

This is how he let me know that in his opinion, the tumor was malignant.

I wanted to get a look at the man who would operate on me and see if I liked him and could trust him. But unless a person is no more than twelve inches from me I see nothing but the contour of head and shoulders. So I went to his desk, braced my hands on it, leaned over and looked at him.

A big, good-looking man of about fifty-five.

He said cheerfully, "You look perfectly fine. How do you feel?"

"I feel perfectly awful," I answered as cheerfully as he, and for this got as much laughter as if it had been brilliant repartee.

I was told later by one of the nurses that he was a Catholic, had five children and went to church everyday before he operated.

I was one of the many patients who were to be operated on that day at the Sibley Hospital. We had been stripped, scrubbed, wrapped in blankets, put into narrow containers that were set upon carts, then wheeled by orderlies to a waiting room which seemed as long as a city block and as noisy as a raucous party.

We were packed in like sardines. It was bedlam. Why all the hilarity? Patients yelling from one bed to another. I could dimly see forms moving—orderlies, nurses, perhaps visitors.

Suddenly there was a small Chinese man beside my bed. He introduced himself and said he was the anesthetist. "I am going to give you a hypodermic, Mrs. Alsop. That's all."

I wondered how he would penetrate the cocoon of

blankets in which I was wrapped, but he was expert. I felt the prick of the needle in my hip.

He went away and after a while I began to feel drowsy. Soon I knew that we were moving. The uproar dimmed.

Then oblivion.

My tumor proved to be a carcinoma, a malignant tumor, but there were no cancerous nodes in the armpit; and the operation was not the end of me for soon I was home again and writing about it.

My recovery was uneventful. I kept the trained nurse for a while. But there was more to come, perhaps the most serious part, explained Dr. Boland. The losing of a bosom was a shock to a woman's psyche. To recover from that, conversations with other women who had had the same experience were available. If I did not want that (I did not) my nurse would take me downtown to a particular shop where there was a particular saleswoman who knew what to do. I went with my nurse, and was measured and fitted and given a "falsie" filled with silicone. For it I shelled out nine crisp ten-dollar bills and got back fifty cents change.

For a woman weighing just one hundred pounds the new bosom seemed unduly bold and aggressive. Besides, it was heavy, and once or twice, when it slipped out of the little pocket that held it in place and out of my overblouse, it hit the floor with quite a thud. So Deirdre went shopping for me at the Bethesda five-and-ten-cent store and found some very light little cones made of foam rubber, one of which I adapted to my dimensions and personality.

After recovery and convalescence one resumes normal life. But nothing seemed normal. Everything felt changed.

The change was in me. I had been traveling in far places and now could not get reoriented—"as a sparrow upon a housetop." But I did not forget what the Bible says about that other sparrow—"Not a sparrow falleth."

I went about the daily chores in my workroom practicing a little, sorting papers, arranging the chapters of this autobiography in a neat pile, when, there, sticking out from under some scripts, was a package with the unmistakable look of a returned manuscript—*The Catch Colt*.

Following our usual procedure, when one publisher returned a manuscript, it was immediately sent to another. *The Catch Colt* had been sent to several. All had returned it. I wondered why. I thought it was a beautiful and interesting story, all about those Wyoming ranch families who live their lives on the very flanks of the Rocky Mountains.

The title, I knew, had always been wrong. It was not of my choosing, but was urged on me by those reporters in Cheyenne. Striking, I admit, taken separately, but a sort of cheat because it was not a horse story like *Flicka*. But because of that word "colt" the public was deceived into thinking it was and then felt disappointed, almost betrayed.

But titles can be changed. People soon forget. And I began to make a list of better, truer titles for this story.

I was not disheartened; I was rather excited. It was like old times having a ship out on the high seas again.

We are waiting and watching for that ship to come in.

34

Show Business

I was questioned incessantly by people about the making of a musical. There was such interest in this subject it seemed to me it needed a book to answer all the questions. So I wrote one.

A Musical in the Making turned out to be a full-length book and, I thought, at least as interesting as the book about "glue." But no publisher would accept it as the play had never got to Broadway. Once again Markane Company stepped in. We had a handsome volume made and the Catholic University immediately made it required reading. Another university followed suit. Then a third. I began to wonder if, perhaps, this odd afterthought of a book might not outlive all my fiction.

As middlemen have a place and function wherever there is buying and selling, there were a number of brokerage houses in New York City that dealt in plays, often plays which had failed to arrive at Broadway but might very well be useful in schools, colleges, and amateur dramatics.

Dramatists Play Service was one of the best of these.

Soon after our return from the Cheyenne production, Kent got in touch with them, but they politely refused us.

My laborious rewriting must have been to some avail, however, since eventually, Dramatists Play Service took us on. This gave the musical an office and address, and would keep it alive.

In the course of time we were notified by Dramatists Play Service that my musical was to be put on by a junior high school in a Maryland town with the unlikely name of Accident. For me, it was exciting news, the culmination of so many years of work. When other people were in charge, how would they interpret and present my characters?

As shows usually begin at eight and we were unfamiliar with the roads to Accident, we decided to make an expedition of it, starting out in the afternoon, taking our time, stopping somewhere on the way for dinner and arriving early.

We had been told Accident was near Cumberland. We found Cumberland on the map and started off at three thirty in the afternoon.

I shall never forget that ride. We got lost, found no place for dinner, the daylight changed to darkness and still we were wandering, pushing blindly forward.

Suddenly we heard a great racket and slowed up. From the edge of the road the ground sloped down into a large basin which was filled with milling cars, crowds of people and off there aways, many lights outlining a long building.

Kent put his head out the window and called, "What's going on here?"

Excited voices shouted, *"The Catch Colt! The Catch Colt!"*

It was as if they were yelling for me. Acclaim! Success! I should have felt triumph. But I felt none.

We parked our car and found seats in the auditorium just as the lights went down and the curtain was lifted.

The performance was a riot. It was ridiculous. It was

the travesty of a play. Yet never was a play more enthusiastically applauded.

The leading part, Letty, was played by a homely child with spectacles who looked small for her age, which I judged to be about twelve. She had a shrill high voice and doubtless got the part because she was able to sing every one of Letty's songs and never missed the beat or the pitch. The character of Windy was played by a boy so tall and thin his schoolmates might have called him the string bean. The part of Joey, actually the star of the production, was marred by the fact that the boy's voice was changing. The role was sung partly in a boy soprano voice and partly in a man's baritone. The conductor, the director, the ringmaster was a woman, a stalwart female who sat at the piano and had eyes, fingers, and voice everywhere.

Speeches which I had written thinking them merely slightly funny got shrieks of laughter.

It began on the dot of eight and ended exactly when it should have. No one broke down in the performance, so of course it must be judged an immense success.

But my artist's soul was outraged. I was wounded to the core.

I saw a series of such performances stretching into the future. I wondered how I had got into this? Well—show business. That was it. And everyone knew it.

I had heard such warnings since childhood. But, as usual, thought I knew best.

Kent was equally disgusted.

When Kent and Deirdre were visiting in England one summer, he investigated theatrical possibilities there. He found conditions which greatly impressed him. Producers, artists, directors, and theaters were closely grouped together. What convenience for anyone working in this field. Moreover, costs were half what they were here.

He talked about *The Catch Colt* to Mr. E. C. Holmes

of the Chappell Music Company and aroused Mr. Holmes's interest. Mr. Holmes agreed to reproduce the music at a price. It meant assembling a musical director, instrumentalists, and singers. Kent gave the order. Of course Hershey Kay's new orchestration would be used.

My next surprise from London was a request for a demonstration tape, and I had to telephone Mike and ask him what such a thing might be.

"You must get a narrator," he explained, "who would tell the story in brief, cutting in parts of the outstanding musical numbers where they belong in the play."

All the cutting would be done at an electronics studio downtown. Mike gave me the address.

But a narrator!

My heart sank. A voice could show insincerity or commonness. How many I would have to audition!

Then I remembered the little transistor radio on its low table before my chair. Trained commentators spoke over the radio all day long. As magically as when, in the fairy story, the fisherman got his wish from the genie in the bottle, I reached out my hand and got my wish. A distinguished voice, with character and brains, answered instantly, "Charles Osgood, 'Newsbreak.'"

It was exactly the right voice.

We wondered if he could do outside work? Kent and Deirdre were now back in this country, and Kent went to the CBS newsroom in New York to get the answer. Yes. Would he do my narration? We put the question to him with a personal letter from me. He answered that he would consider it an honor to be associated with Mary O'Hara, and asked for information about the narration.

I had a sketch ready to send him, the tale of the half-cracked old fellow who haunted the sheep camps and called himself a sheepherder, though he had once been a professor at Harvard University. He was a long-winded character and would begin to lecture at a moment's notice, telling everyone he was hunting a little boy, "about so high, a tow-head, with blue eyes, my grandson." Born and bred, married and widowed in Cambridge, Massachusetts, he had raised his son Joseph to follow in his steps. But the boy had a violent temper and very different ideas. They had many altercations. One day Joseph dropped out of college and ran away, and got married. A year later a letter came from Windemere, Wyoming, saying that the young wife had died in childbirth, the baby was a boy. Joseph had named him after his father, Joseph Gerard Willoughby, III.

This did not mollify the professor, but he carefully wrote the date and name in the family Bible, thinking, now, of course he will come home and expect me to take them in. He determined to do so. He would forgive Joseph. But Joseph did not come. He did not even write again.

A few years later the professor himself fell ill and when he recovered he retired from his teaching job and decided he would go west, find his son and grandson and bring them home.

But when he got to Windemere, which was a little town in the sheep-raising country, he found that his son had died there of Rocky Mountain spotted fever a few years before.

He could find out nothing about the child, though he visited all the ranches and sheep camps nearby. People answered kindly his persistent questions. He described the child as if he had seen him. And in time, he came to feel that he had.

Walking the Wyoming plains he regained his health and strength. He came to rejoice in the freedom of it and the beauty of the world about him. The search for the child became a way of life, a pattern. Windy was now a notable in that part of Wyoming, a personage, someone to be observed with respect, the tall spare frame crowned with bushy, upstanding white hair and always fastidiously dressed.

And so, while Windy hunted for his grandson, the boy grew tall and strong, skillful with livestock, with the handling of horses, with all the work that went with ranching.

The old man was held by his dream, spellbound. So they passed each other, these two, sometimes quite close, but never knowing that what they sought was theirs for the taking, the old man his grandson, the young man—a family, a home, and a name.

The story must have pleased Mr. Osgood, for he replied immediately, saying that he would do it.

I had lived through the silent movies with the speech printed above the scene; through movies with an offstage speaker dubbing in the words; and then, at last, through movies with the actor himself speaking the words. And now this: songs sung in London; Charles Osgood narrating in New York; myself arranging the cutting and splicing together of pieces of tape in Washington. With all this I can cross the room from where I am sitting and typing to my record player in the opposite corner, put on my demonstration tape and hear a microcosm of my whole show.

There is not as much time in a year as there used to be. I have found that out. People accept the mysterious behavior of time thoughtlessly, with casual remarks such as: "The hour dragged endlessly," or, "The whole week was gone in a flash." But there are wiser words in Isaiah: What is to come is now. And what has been, still is.

Surely that tells us that there is no such thing as *time*. We have invented it to fit our clocks and calendars and help us keep our engagements.

At last I sent a copy of the finished demonstration tape to Mike for his appraisal and waited in great suspense. He telephoned me, "Mary, it is gorgeous!"

How sweet is praise!

Rachmaninoff, the famous pianist and composer, said, "An artist needs three things. Praise. And Praise. And Praise."

And since the first two words of the doxology are "Praise God," He must like it, too.

35

My Companions

Earlier in my life, had I been asked about my companions, there would have been a long list. But as one progresses down the years, the list grows smaller, there are fewer and fewer. I can name them now in one short sentence: Kent, my son; Deirdre, my daughter-in-law; Hosannah Faison, who comes once a week to clean my house and who has done that for twenty-two years; and Missy, a small calico cat who has two large gray spots on her otherwise white body and a long gray tail.

That is, these four are my only living companions. But inanimate objects can be companions too, like my piano and my typewriter. In fact, this whole house and garden.

From where I sit typing, I move in thought from this room to the house to the block, and realize why the street was named Grove Street, for it must have been cut, originally, out of a small forest. In places, the leafy tops of the original trees are still waving—the sassafras trees are the tallest, though fragile and short-lived. In other places they have been replaced with handsomer specimens, perhaps oaks, or hemlocks to intertwine their branches and define and enclose the garden.

I bought this place, moved to Washington to be near Kent and Deirdre and their children. Their house is just across the street from mine. Can that have been thirteen years ago?

This particular block of Grove Street has some unusual features. It has no sidewalk. The tree-shaded houses stand on higher ground than the curbstones and the front lawns slope down to it quite abruptly in places. The houses are mostly white, or plastered white over pink brick, and the roof lines are irregular, dropping at one end a half story for a two-car garage. In the convenient modern manner the garage is attached to the house.

In my house the space over the two-car garage made a mezzanine of considerable size which was broken up into smaller rooms. I had some remodeling done. I tore out all those partitions and made the whole space into one large room, a room long enough to hold the double-B Mason and Hamlin grand piano, a large sofa, a corner for this typewriter, chair and tables, another corner for a bookcase that would go from floor to ceiling, another corner for my hi-fi and loudspeaker, the last corner filled with shelves for my music and compositions. Windows on north, east, and south. Walls painted pale gray, dark polished floors.

When I first put the room together I had trouble with the windows. There ought to be no curtains to muffle the wonderful tones of the piano, and the room had the exciting empty look of a room that exists to be lived and worked in. But the reverberations were unbearably loud. They had to be muffled. I hung long curtains, from ceiling to floor at the six windows. They were a beautiful red, not scarlet or crimson, but blood red. Then I found I could not work in the room, could hardly look into it, and finally realized I was even ashamed of it.

I changed them to horizon blue curtains and the room

was at rest, ready to go to work in. It makes me happy just to step into it every morning and shut the door behind me.

Now that I have lost so much vision and hearing, a mental life is what remains to me. The mind's eye. The mind's ear. How fortunate that that is where I have put my riches.

In the mind's eye is preserved the scene of the frozen bluebirds. At a flick of my will I can see it again—the floor of the barn littered with the tiny blue bodies, all lying on their backs; how we had gathered them up and carried them to the house; the way they had come to life in the warm kitchen and flown through all the rooms; then at last when we had opened the windows their swoops out to the sunlight and freedom.

The mind's ear? Equally generous with its gifts, I glance across the room from where I am typing and see the shape of the Mason and Hamlin against the north wall of the room. The look of a concert grand piano, the shape of it, the length of the strings that reach from the keyboard to the long narrow point, has all sorts of associations for me: the concerts I've heard, the great virtuosos who have performed impossibly beautiful things. Even Paderewski.

At will I can listen to the performance of any of the great symphonies; I can stretch out on the sofa and order the program. My favorites, the ones best known to me, are performed with exquisite detail. Melodies. Harmonies. Dynamics. And if I want the actual sound I have the records and a wonderful hi-fi. Or I can go to the piano myself, play the common chord and let its promise, its peace and calm, fill the room. So my music room is filled with concerts and panoramas.

Of my four living companions, I'll begin with Missy because that will include a good deal of Kent. I have an affinity for cats. They are thoroughly adult, not like dogs, who remain children forever. I understand them, can talk to them and they reciprocate with the most intense affection. They go for walks with me either short or long; they try always to be as near to me as they can. At first sight of me they never fail to greet me.

There has been a long procession of them: Tilly, Fritzi, McGinty, Micky, Pauly, and now Missy. Taking care of an animal is like taking care of a child. Missy is never entirely out of my thoughts. I know about where she is, what she is doing, and have a thought for her next feeding time. She has an astonishing vocabulary. We have many conversations and understand each other perfectly.

When Kent comes in the evening to see me, he has a game with Missy. He frightens her, makes horrible sounds, stamps his feet and pretends to attack her. Missy vanishes. When he leaves, and the front door slams behind him, she emerges, runs to me and whispers, "Has he gone?"

But they are great friends. When he rakes the leaves in the garden and a wind springs up making them lift and swirl, she is there with him, leaping and whirling and batting the leaves with her paws. "She's like a kitten," Kent says.

Indoors, he picks her up and sets her on his knee. "Now you come here to your daddy."

During the night she is in the garden if weather permits, and has a way to get into the garage in case it rains. But she prefers to get thoroughly drenched and have me give her a rub down. She has a special big red bath towel. I sit on the kitchen floor and maul her and tumble her. No matter how rough I am or what part of her I grip she comes back for more. And loud purring fills the room.

Cats' lives are tragic. Their deaths are apt to be sudden in towns or cities, almost killed or half killed by cars hitting them.

I remember the day when I went down to the kitchen to make my breakfast and there was no little Missy waiting at the door to be let in to breakfast with me. I went about my business, looking out the door every few minutes,

worried, anxious but not believing that she would not be
there in a moment.

And she was. But what was the matter with her?
What was she dragging behind her? I rushed out and ran to
her. She was just inching along. A cluster of strings were
tied around her chest and attached to a bush which she was
dragging behind her as she struggled home. The strings
were tied in a slipknot on her chest, so tightly that they cut
into her. As she had pulled the bush out by the roots to get
away, every inch she pulled tightened the noose.

As I cut the bonds and took her in my arms she
collapsed, purring. For a week she could hardly move.

It was a mystery. Children could not have tied such a
slipknot. But who but children would be so cruel?

What charms me so about Missy is the way she has
linked her day's activity with mine. When I do my floor
exercises, she walks around and around me, not touching
me. She always knows what time it is. When I am typing,
she comes to me at lunch and tells me it is time to stop and
come down. She has the counterpoint to every part I play, a
sort of *pas de deux*. We are partners in a dance. To have an
accompanist so expert and so original to accompany all my
monotonous daily chores throws a bright light on all my
doings.

"Hosie, why did Jesus Christ have to go down to
Hades after he was crucified?"

"To put down the devil and all his works."

Hosannah, my house cleaner, carries with her wherever she goes a shopping bag which holds inside it a good-
sized Bible. She has told me that on the few occasions when
she left for work and forgot to take the Bible she had to go
back and get it. She would have been lonesome all day
without it.

If she can't sleep at night, she sometimes gets up and
sits in a chair with her Bible, but not to read, just to hold

in her lap. She says there is a spirit in her Bible that sustains her and speaks to her.

When I told her that my breast sometimes hurts—the one they cut off—she told me that was because they didn't bury it. They just threw it away.

Hosie weighs more than twice what I do but is put out when her doctor tells her that she is eating too much and must reduce. "I'm fixin to bake me a cake Saturday mornin'," she told my granddaughter, "and ain't nobody gonna stop me."

I wonder if Hosie won't find the end before I do.

I am so beholden to Deirdre, my daughter-in-law, that I am often ashamed. I couldn't do without her. She shops for me, reads my fan mail to me, keeps track of my appointments, in fact often thinks for me.

When I first met her I perceived her strength and said to Kent that she could run a girls' school or, in fact, an army. Not at all what Kent cared to hear. What he saw in her was a pretty and petite female, a gay chatterbox with beguiling childish ways, wholly desirable.

But Kent had strength too. He could be immovable. What would happen when they locked horns? I need not have worried. It has been a wonderful marriage without the slightest sign of their ever having regretted it. She looks the same as when she married him. Hasn't changed by a hair.

Deirdre hurries into my hospital room carrying cardboard boxes full of dresses.

"We're going to a dance tonight and I want to wear a new dress. Which one should I wear?"

I prop up my head while she models them. One. Two. Three.

"Now again," I order.

At last I pick one and she packs them up and hurries away.

One time she rushed into my house yelling, "Your house is on fire and smoke is pouring out of all your windows."

In no time at all Grove Street was full of fire engines, trucks, hook and ladders, and my house was full of helmeted firemen who looked to me to be seven feet tall. They carried all sorts of tools, big cylinders, and were draped with coils of fire hose.

It was not my fault. Kent and Deirdre, to safeguard me, had installed a system of smoke detectors in the house. All I did was bake a cheese mixture for my lunch. When it was done, I turned off the fire, took the tiny casserole out of the oven, and in so doing spilled about a half tablespoonful on the bottom of the oven. As it lay there, sizzling, it smoked.

I was eating my lunch in the dining room when the excitement began. As it progressed I chose a comfortable armchair in the corner of the living room. I was properly dressed in white linen slacks and tunic. Of course there was nothing I could do. I was glad to see that everyone seemed to enjoy it. In fact, all Grove Street enjoyed it.

One thing more about Deirdre and Kent is the pleasure they can take in dancing with each other. Yes. After the many years of married life, they can turn to each other when the music begins and be "swept away."

I remember one night they told me about an unusually good dance band. Since my social pleasures are now all vicarious, this was delightful to hear. I drifted back in thought. Where would I stop? There was a memory I was trying to catch—ah, yes, Colonel Watling and that "little b___, Molly Parrot."

36

Past, Present, Future

Except for possibly a post-script such as one adds to a letter, this will be the last chapter of my autobiography. It is the length I intended; and I am tired of writing it.

But besides tying up a few loose ends, I want, if I can, to sum up the religious journey which has accompanied my earthly peregrinations.

I began as an Episcopalian, then moved into the wilderness of older Hindu religions before a return to Christianity, this time into the Roman Catholic Church. When people ask me why I took that last step, I tell them it was because I love the saints, who in the Protestant church seem to attract so little attention. It is as if a musician should pay little attention to Beethoven, Tchaikovsky, Mozart, Bach.

I think Mr. Burnell disapproved of my becoming a Catholic. Arcadia was church enough; his lectures, sermons enough.

But it was, in fact, he himself who had inclined me in that direction, when, one summer, he began to lecture on the early Christian fathers, and I bought the books and devoured them. It was one of the great experiences of my life when those books came into my house. Books on St. John of the Cross. Books by St. Augustine, St. Teresa of Avila, and the great teacher, St. Thomas Aquinas. More wonderful companions for my declining years. But how steep that declivity and to what depth it reaches is never known to us, which is a pity, because one never knows whether to be beginning something or just marking time and waiting.

All my generation has long since died. My friends Ethel and Nan and Fanny; my teachers, Mr. Burnell and Vernon Spencer; my siblings, except my astounding sister Elma, who is four years older than I and wants to be a hundred. I do not. But she can read. I can not. I envy her that. The only way I have been able to write the last half of this autobiography is through my knowledge of the touch system of typing. I type a few pages blindly. In the evening when Kent comes over to visit me, he reads back to me what I have written so I can correct and revise it as many times as is needed.

I am not just marking time. I could not do that. It would be too boring. Besides, no prolific writer comes to the end of one piece without another—sometimes two or three—already taking shape in his mind.

That is all I have to tell. As for the postscript, I can tell it right here, because I remember it perfectly.

One day when the past history of the city of Los Angeles was news, because it was celebrating an anniversary, *Newsweek* carried an article that concerned me and all my descendants.

It stated, in brief, that in an era when the wealthy cities of the country were being ravaged by Al Capone and his gangsters, Los Angeles had been protected by a political genius, Kent K. Parrot. This political genius was my gentle son's father, my first husband. As I remember the article, Capone and his gang did descend on Los Angeles, with intent to ravage, but the political genius did battle with them and put them to flight. In fact, he bounced them. Genius! *Newsweek*'s report elated me.

The episode should have given him fame instead of notoriety, but there were many people in California who still believed that he was in the same class with the other political bosses of big cities. I felt that all the Pro boys yet to come should know about it. So I carefully cut the article out of the magazine to save it for my son and give it to him one day. Now is the time, and I can think of no better way to tell him of it than right here in my autobiography.

CHRISTIAN HERALD ASSOCIATION AND ITS MINISTRIES

CHRISTIAN HERALD ASSOCIATION, founded in 1878, publishes The Christian Herald Magazine, one of the leading interdenominational religious monthlies in America. Through its wide circulation, it brings inspiring articles and the latest news of religious developments to many families. From the magazine's pages came the initiative for CHRISTIAN HERALD CHILDREN'S HOME and THE BOWERY MISSION, two individually supported not-for-profit corporations.

CHRISTIAN HERALD CHILDREN'S HOME, established in 1894, is the name for a unique and dynamic ministry to disadvantaged children, offering hope and opportunities which would not otherwise be available for reasons of poverty and neglect. The goal is to develop each child's potential and to demonstrate Christian compassion and understanding to children in need.

Mont Lawn is a permanent camp located in Bushkill, Pennsylvania. It is the focal point of a ministry which provides a healthful "vacation with a purpose" to children who without it would be confined to the streets of the city. Up to 1000 children between the ages of 7 and 11 come to Mont Lawn each year.

Christian Herald Children's Home maintains year-round contact with children by means of an *In-City Youth Ministry*. Central to its philosophy is the belief that only through sustained relationships and demonstrated concern can individual lives be truly enriched. Special emphasis is on individual guidance, spiritual and family counseling and tutoring. This follow-up ministry to inner-city children culminates for many in financial assistance toward higher education and career counseling.

THE BOWERY MISSION, located at 227 Bowery, New York City, has since 1879 been reaching out to the lost men on the Bowery, offering them what could be their last chance to rebuild their lives. Every man is fed, clothed and ministered to. Countless numbers have entered the 90-day residential rehabilitation program at the Bowery Mission. A concentrated ministry of counseling, medical care, nutrition therapy, Bible study and Gospel services awakens a man to spiritual renewal within himself.

These ministries are supported solely by the voluntary contributions of individuals and by legacies and bequests. Contributions are tax deductible. Checks should be made out either to CHRISTIAN HERALD CHILDREN'S HOME or to THE BOWERY MISSION.

Administrative Office: 40 Overlook Drive, Chappaqua, New York 10514
Telephone: (914) 769-9000

DATE DUE